UNITY AND SCHISM

BY THE
Rev. T. A. LACEY, M.A.

*The Bishop Paddock Lectures
for 1917*

A. R. MOWBRAY & CO. Ltd.
LONDON : 28 Margaret Street, Oxford Circus, W.
OXFORD : 9 High Street
MILWAUKEE, U.S.A. : The Young Churchman Co.

First impression, 1917

ANGLIS

HOSPITIBVS . AMERICANIS

TANQVAM . IN . PATRIA . MORATVS

HOSPES . BRITANNICVS

ANGLVS

PREFACE

THE Bishop Paddock Lectures are delivered annually in the Chapel of the General Theological Seminary at New York. When the Trustees of the foundation honoured me with an invitation to undertake the course for the year 1916–17, the Dean of the Seminary suggested that I might with advantage lecture on the Unity of the Church and the effects of Schism. I gladly adopted the suggestion. The subject is one which insistently demands attention. Concurrent with a growing toleration of the divisions of Christendom is an active and widespread movement towards Christian union. The combination is curious. Men who are unwilling to speak of schism, who resent plain speaking about it, and accept its present consequences as if they were a normal feature of the Christian religion, press forward eagerly in search of a plan for modifying or even terminating a state of things to which they seem to have little objection in principle. There are dangers in this course of action. To make

v

disunion the starting-point, to seek union
without condemning schism, or to condemn
its manifestations only on the ground of
expediency, is to pin one's faith to a purely
human scheme, and to aim at a result purely
artificial. In criticism of this habit of thought
I have tried to ascertain what is the natural
unity given to the Church by the purpose and
act of God. It is an investigation of what is,
not of what may be. There are positive theories
to be tested, and negations to be examined.
Unity and schism are correlatives. We cannot
properly understand a rending, and still less
can we repair the rents, without knowing the
nature of the fabric that is torn.

I fear I may seem rather rash than courageous
when I criticize the dominating theories on
which the various sections of Christendom
have built their practice, finding flaws or
insufficiencies in all alike. In case of need
I can defend myself, observing that in point
of fact the working of these theories has
produced precisely that state of things which
is universally deplored. But indeed I trust
that in criticizing them I have not contradicted
anything which is taught by the whole Catholic
Church, and that I have treated with due

respect what is taught or done even by any
part of the Church. At any rate my temerity
has not carried me to the length of proposing
any reconstruction of existing systems.

I have thought it well to add to my Lectures
appendices containing important documents in
illustration of the theories examined. Quotations from St. Cyprian I have woven into a
connected argument ; the rest I leave for the
most part to tell their own tale. Some readers
will probably be glad to have the complete
text of the dogmatic decree of the Fourth
Session of the Vatican Council. In some
respects it would be more satisfactory to
substitute the Encyclical *Satis cognitum* of
Leo XIII ; but this seems to be in a less
degree authoritative, and the use made of
some patristic quotations — *pace tanti uiri
dixerim* — is so strange and forced that its
detailed argument is even less persuasive than
the curtness of the conciliar exposition.

I am indebted to my friend and neighbour,
the Rev. J. H. Shakespeare, for a copy of the
Interim Reports of the Committees appointed
by the Mansfield College Conference of last
year, and to the Rev. F. J. Hall, D.D., one of
my kind hosts at the General Seminary, for

calling my attention to the Resolution of the American Bishops cited in Appendix VI, as also for some useful criticisms passed on the Lectures at the time of their delivery. By these I have profited in revising the Lectures for the press, but for the most part they are printed as they were delivered.

I was visiting the United States at a critical moment in the history of my own country and of all mankind. I found there friends of a generosity which surpassed my expectations, though these were by no means narrowly conceived. I found sympathy with us in our trials, a kindly judgement of our faults, a warm-hearted appreciation of our aims. The rapid movement of events that began shortly after my arrival produced in addition a readiness to share our burdens. While returning home, in the region of danger at sea, I heard that the die was cast and our friends were become our allies. Old discords pass; old kinships revive. The event fits my theme.

It is a poor sort of display to mention books which have been found useful. Indeed, I could hardly do it. The reading of a lifetime, all too desultory, has gone to the making of these Lectures; if the result is unsatisfactory,

I must bear the responsibility alone. Two recent books, however, I will name. One contains the stimulating lectures of a predecessor on the same foundation. When Dr. Figgis speaks of *The Fellowship of the Mystery*, it is good to listen. The other is the Bishop of Zanzibar's formless but appealing discourse, *The Fulness of Christ*. This came into my hands when I was preparing the last of my Lectures. I had been working hard at controversial criticism, and my soul was dried up for want of fatness. The Bishop of Zanzibar poured the unction of the Spirit into my subject. I have lifted his pregnant remark that we ought to make the unity of the Church a matter rather of religion than of theology. What else I owe to him is not easily said.

It is right to mention the fact—however unimportant—that I have incorporated into these Lectures the substance of a sermon preached before the University of Oxford, on November 5, 1916, and published in the *English Church Review* of April, 1917.

b

CONTENTS

———

LECTURE I

LECTURE II

Contents

LECTURE III

LECTURE IV

LECTURE V

LECTURE VI

LECTURE VII

APPENDICES

UNITY AND SCHISM

LECTURE I

THE FUNDAMENTAL IDEA

There is one body and one Spirit, even as ye also were
called in one hope of your calling ; one Lord, one faith,
one baptism, one God and Father of all, who is over all,
and through all, and in all.—*Eph.* iv. 4.

WE declare our belief in one Holy Catholic
Church, and about this general conception of oneness there is hardly any dispute
among Christians. True : but about the implications of the idea there are many questions.
Do we speak of a mere numerical unit, the
Church of Christ being one, and not many, or
are we to understand also that this one Church
is a close union ? Has it a social unity ? If so,
what is the nature of this unity ? Is it an ideal
unity, towards which we are moving through
manifold divisions while the people of God is

B

slowly gathered together ; or is it a real unity
subsisting from the first ? Is it a purely spiritual
unity of men consciously or unconsciously
serving the same Master and living by the
same gifts of grace, or is it a corporate unity,
an organized body of men visibly bound
together by common beliefs, practices, and
traditions ? Is the maintenance of this unity
a counsel of perfection, or is it a necessary
law ? If it be necessary, what kind of necessity
is understood ? Is it a necessity of existence,
so that a divided Church would be no Church
at all, and an undivided Church must be dis-
coverable if the promise of God has not come
to naught ; or is it a moral necessity, something required for the fulfilment of the purpose
of God, which human perversity can never-
theless withhold ? In either case, is there
required a kind of union that will be evident to
a superficial observer, clear and unmistakable,
or will a deeper kind of union suffice, under-
lying divisions conspicuous on the surface ?
A familiar illustration, drawn from another
field of thought, may serve to show the value
of these distinctions. There was but one Italy,
when the peninsula was divided into a number
of separate states ; this one Italy was, in

a measure, united ; there was a certain unity
of language, unity of tradition, unity of senti-
ment, unity of national feeling ; of a different
kind, but hardly more complete, is the unity of
the kingdom to-day.   What kind of unity is
the unity of the Church ?

Since the Church is recognized, ideally at
least, as one, it follows that divisions among
Christians are at least a grave cause for anxiety.
It is evident that one kind of division is not to
be thought of.   A division which would have
the effect of making not one Church, but two
or more Churches, will be impossible.   If such
division appear, it will not mean that the
Church is divided ; one part alone will be the
true Church, and others will be false pretenders
to the title.   But, on the other hand, some
kinds of division are universally allowed as
necessary and useful.   How shall we distinguish
between what is harmful and what is good ?
What is the effect of harmful divisions ?
Every case must be considered on its merits.
Does the Church remain one, though divided ;
or is a party separated entirely from the Church,
which thus maintains undivided unity in the
majority—or the minority—remaining faithful ?

These are the fundamental questions to

which I address myself. To these, and to
some others arising immediately out of them,
I hope to confine myself.

There is "one Body." We are so accustomed
to the use of the phrase in this connection that
we are inclined to give it a necessary implication
of social order. But this seems to be a mistake.
I cannot trace any such use of the Greek word,
though it was familiar in the case of the Latin
corpus. When St. Paul called the Church the
Body of Christ, it is improbable that he had in
his mind what we mean when we speak of
incorporation. Indications of social order must
be sought elsewhere at the beginning. There
is no lack of them. I shall not undertake here
to examine the theories of Rudolf Sohm. It
has been sufficiently done. I am content to
observe that even he regards the development
of discipleship into an organized community as
inevitable from the first. From the first, and
speedily, he sees the Church growing into
a social order, with officers and regulations, and
even with a financial system. It is this society
that St. Paul calls the Body of Christ, and you
may note that among the diverse members of
the Body is included " he that ruleth." [1]   The

[1] Rom. xii. 8.

tradition from the beginning hasıbeen constant.
Even those who have abandoned belief in
a tangible organization of the whole Church,
looking rather to an invisible unity of the faithful in the Body of Christ, attach undiminished
importance to those visible Churches which
they regard as imperfect images of the ideal.
Social order, social organization, is conspicuous
everywhere ; if it were of later and slower
growth than we know it to have been, we
might still see in it the working of a divine
purpose, a necessary element in Christianity.
The figure of the one Body is illuminating ;
in the religion of the Incarnation you may
expect to find an articulated habitation of the
one Spirit.

If this corporate unity is necessary, we shall
know what to say of divisions. There are
divisions, articulations, which do not destroy
unity, but are rather needed for its perfection.
There are divisions which endanger unity.
St. Paul has named them ; they are σχίσματα,
rendings of the Body. There are, I suppose,
no Christians who do not condemn schism ;
they differ only in determining what it
is, or in fixing the shame of it on one
another.

Let us go back to the beginning. Dimly we perceive the apostolic fellowship. It is drawn for us by St. Luke with a few bold strokes, thoroughly artistic. We can see that here is no formal history, no minute inquiry into sources. It is a memory. The state of things depicted has already passed away, and the narrator is interested in what survives ; he cares only to show the origins of the Church that he knows, the Church of his companionship with St. Paul. He selects what is good for this purpose. Do not complain that he writes for edification. He writes for nothing else. He is neither abstract historian nor laborious annalist. But there is history in his narrative, and to some extent you can see the disciples of Jesus as they appeared to their neighbours ; as they appeared, perhaps, to themselves. They are apparently a sect of Jews. If Judaism be a polity, they are included ; if it be a religion, they are of it, but with a difference. They hold its beliefs, they observe its precepts, they share its worship. These are illumined by a new hope, a new consciousness of spiritual power ; above all, by a conviction that the Messiah has come, has died, has risen from the dead, and is now reigning, not the less in reality if out of sight.

There is more in their belief in Jesus, but the more is not yet conspicuous.

They are a sect within Judaism, but they are moving towards the circumference. There is a tendency to separate. Do not say that all sects tend to separation. It is not true, or nations would be rent in pieces by political parties. But it is true of these sectaries. There is something in their principles that will divide them from the rest of the Jews. Their position within will be untenable, should they wish to retain it. There are two difficulties. They have a message for mankind, not for one nation alone, and their own nation is jealous of strangers. They have a passionate belief in their Lord as the King of Israel, and how can they hold communion with Israel that denies Him ? There is a tendency to separation, of which they slowly become conscious.

They become conscious of something else, and perhaps more speedily. They are making a new departure, even within the circle of Judaism. They have been nurtured on Messianic hopes that were exclusively national, and yet pointed to a mission of the nation to the whole world. To some extent, perhaps, acquaintance with the methods of the Roman

Empire fashioned their expectation of the Kingdom of God that was to be. There is nothing to show that their Master corrected those expectations in detail. He laid down fruitful principles, and gave obscure indications of method ; but to the last day of their intercourse with Him they could still ask in the old style whether He would at once restore the kingdom to Israel. So far they are on familiar ground.

Yet, in spite of bewilderment and disappointment, they are convinced that great things are being done. Messianic hopes are already being fulfilled ; the Kingdom is in the act of being established. They rely on a return of their Lord from heaven, which they picture for themselves in the old apocalyptic colours ; but even now He is with them here in power, and their seat of government is with Him in heaven.

Here is something new. Their movement within Judaism is not a movement of reform. They do not call men back to the observance of precepts neglected or of principles forgotten. They do not aim, like Ezekiel or Ezra, at an ideal reconstruction of the past. Their eyes are fixed on the future. Their aspirations will find apocalyptic expression in terms of a new heaven and a new earth.

In the books of the old prophets of reformation, however, there is found an idea that will determine the form of their new departure. The doctrine of the Faithful Remnant is adumbrated in the story of Elijah, where the seven thousand who have not bowed the knee to Baal represent the true Israel that will survive a general apostasy. It appears expressly in the teaching of Isaiah during the storm of Assyrian conquest : " The remnant that is escaped of the house of Judah shall yet again take root downward and bear fruit upward." Ethical values are here in the background. They become prominent in the prophecies of the next great catastrophic period, the Babylonian captivity, which is treated as a day of winnowing. Once become explicit, the doctrine is used in the prophetic presentation of history from the beginning ; it accounts for the call of Abraham out of Haram ; it gives a meaning to the rejection of Ishmael and of Esau. It is a doctrine of continuous narrowing ; there is always a falling away, but always a remnant which stands firm, to continue the holy seed.

It is impossible to say how soon the disciples

c

of Jesus Christ began to apply this prophetic
teaching to their own case. The application
was not long delayed, and it was general. It
is implicit in the address of the Epistle of
St. James. He is certainly writing to disciples,
and he calls them "the twelve tribes in the
Dispersion," a designation which implies that
they constitute the true Israel. It becomes
explicit in the Epistle to the Romans, where
St. Paul's argument is not only that the
Gentiles are brought into the inheritance of
the promise, but also that the greater part of
Israel, for the time being at least, is falling
away. "Not all those who are of Israel are
Israel;" a remnant only will be saved "according to the election of grace." The same thought
underlies the address of the First Epistle of
St. Peter to "elect sojourners of the Dispersion." It is implied in the New Jerusalem
of the Apocalypse, where the nations are
gathered to the true Israel, and it may serve
to account for those at Smyrna "who say they
are Jews, and are not."

Here we see the significance of the word
Ecclesia, as derived from the Greek of the
Septuagint. I shall bow to the authority of
Hort in acknowledging that we do not know

how much this term meant for Jews of the
Dispersion,[1] but in the later books of the Old
Testament it clearly stood for the people of
Israel regarded as a community acting together
under recognized chiefs. When the disciples
of Jesus Christ called themselves the Ecclesia
of God, they declared themselves to be the
faithful remnant, the true Israel. Their new
departure was not the creation of a new people,
a new society ; it was a continuation under
new conditions of the Ecclesia of the Old
Testament.

St. Paul carries the doctrine of the Remnant
further. The Jews were the seed of Abraham,
to which the promise was made. But no, he
says, their claim must be disallowed. With
daring treatment of a text, he insists on the
singularity of the seed ; the Jews are many,
therefore they are not the seed ; the one
Christ is the Seed to which the promise was
made. "He saith not, And to seeds, as of
many, but as of one ; And to thy seed, which is
Christ." So the remnant is reduced to one.
You may find fault with St. Paul's exegesis,
but do not shut your eyes to the sublimity of
his thought. His thought is this : Jesus Christ

[1] *The Christian Ecclesia*, p. 7.

Himself is the Remnant, the true seed of
Abraham ; Jesus born of Mary, and by legal
right the Son of David, is more than a repre-
sentative of Israel ; He is the whole of Israel,
all that is left. "They all forsook Him and
fled." Jesus bearing witness before Caiaphas,
Jesus derelict upon the Cross, is the Faithful
Remnant. From Him begins the new expansion
of the people of God. The Church is gathered
to Christ, and is in Christ. It is plain to see
why St. Paul called it the Body of Christ.

Numerical unity has little meaning until it
is set over against multiplicity ; social unity is
not much in evidence until it is in peril of
dissolution. Upon the Church of the first age
there was forced a problem of unity in both
senses. It was in imminent danger of becoming
not one, but many ; if one, it was threatened
with a social cleavage. The difficulty began
with the admission of Gentile converts. How
did they stand in relation to the true Israel ?
In their most exclusive days the Jews had
been willing to receive proselytes, but not
without safeguards ; there were various degrees
of approach, and not until the last barrier
was passed might the proselyte of justice be
accounted an Israelite indeed. Were these

distinctions to be perpetuated ? Were Gentile
converts to be proselytes, or were they at
once to be incorporated with equal rights and
duties in the Christian society ? This question
was inevitable. There was a further question
which might have been avoided. Were these
converts, when fully admitted, to observe
the Mosaic Law ? Since the Church of the
New Testament was continuous with the
Church of the Old Testament this might
be expected. Moreover, the leaders of the
Church, and their first adherents, were all
bound, by an obligation from which they had
no thought of escaping, to the observance of
that Law ; this being so, its rules prevented
them from living in unrestricted intercourse
with others who did not observe it ; if Gentile
converts ignored it, they would be a class
apart. There were good reasons for continuing
the observance, and for binding it upon all.
But from the first the Gentile converts appear
to have been recalcitrant. How could division
be avoided ?

We connect the name of St. Paul with this
question, but it was evidently stirred before
he became prominent. Its origin is definitely
referred to St. Peter. Following upon his first

bold step there are traces of divided counsels,
of reaction, of compromise.   In the Epistle
to the Galatians, Peter is roundly accused of
unworthy accommodation to prejudice.   A
hard word is used—he played the hypocrite.[1]
St. Paul wrote this in burning anger.   The
question was for him one of principle.   Yet
he himself felt the pressure of a difficulty
about the Law.   He asserted his own freedom,
and not only that of his Gentile converts ; yet
on some occasions he observed the Law, even
while he was declaring it obsolete.   He too
could be accommodating.   He avows it : "To
the Jews I became as a Jew, that I might gain
Jews : to them that are under the Law, as
under the Law, not being myself under the
Law, that I might gain them that are under
the Law."   He had recovered his temper, if
I may so say, and could now tolerate in a
measure the very thing that he had denounced
at Antioch.   Evidently there was a very
difficult question.

The peril of disruption was great, and it
was necessary to walk warily.   The importance
attached by St. Paul to the maintenance of
unity is shown by the price that he was

[1] Συνυπεκρίθησαν.—Gal. ii. 13.

willing to pay for it. He would put up with any compromise which did not mean the abandonment of the principle for which he was contending. To avoid offence, he would himself do things against which he revolted. He warned the Galatians that if they received circumcision Christ would profit them nothing, yet in their very midst he had Timothy circumcised, when taking him for a companion, " because of the Jews that were in those parts." He would run some risk even of imperilling the faith, rather than break up the unity of the Church.

Two kinds of disruption were in sight. In the first place, the strict observance of the Mosaic Law by Jewish disciples would make it impossible for them to live on terms of perfect social unity with Gentile converts. A local Church would thus be divided ; a local schism would be established. But the effect would be more than local. What is fine and fruitful in Sohm's treatment of Christian origins is the observation that local Churches were not so many separate organizations ; every particular gathering of disciples was in some sort the whole Church. The King was there in their midst, unseen ; and where

He was all was.   If, therefore, Christians
living in the same place could not meet
together because of some sharp dividing line,
there would be two Churches, not one ; Christ
would be divided.

To take the measure of the difficulty you
have but to remember that a strict observance
of the Law, as commonly understood, would
prevent a Jewish Christian from sharing a
common meal with Gentile converts.   The
Agape, whatever it may have been, would fall
to pieces, and a common Eucharist would
probably be impossible.   This, we can hardly
doubt, was the trouble at Antioch when Peter,
" fearing them that were of the circumcision,"
drew back from his practice of eating with
Gentiles.   But without the common meal, in
whatever degree sacred, the community of the
Church was lost.   In his interview with the
elder Apostles at Jerusalem St. Paul seems to
have accepted a distinction of mission ; they
should go to the Circumcision, he to the
Gentiles ; but when this distinction was extended to the point of dividing a local Church
he vehemently withstood them.   This was not
" according to the truth of the Gospel."
There was to be one communion and fellow-

ship. There were only two ways in which it could be achieved. Either the Gentiles must strictly observe the Law, or the Jews must give up their strict observance. The former alternative was intolerable, and was already put aside by the Apostles at Jerusalem. The latter remained ; the Law must give way to the need of unity.

But there was a larger question. The distinction of mission was not without its dangers. In Jerusalem and Judæa there were Churches entirely Jewish, clinging to the observance of the Law, continuing in attendance at the worship at the Temple, offering the sacrifices of the Old Testament. We have a glimpse of St. Paul at Jerusalem conforming to their practice, undergoing the right of purification made necessary by his contact with Gentiles. James and the presbyters urge this upon him, and he consents. We can imagine his reluctance, the touch of conscience in doing a thing so much at variance with his teaching. We may even conjecture that he would have some joy in the failure of this scheme of conciliation, in the scene of riotous uproar that ensued, and in the consequent peril of his life. Once more he had become as a Jew

D

to the Jews, that he might gain Jews, and the
Jews would have none of him. The Sanhedrim
saw clearer than James. This new thing was
to be the end of the old. The two were
irreconcilable. For the Jewish Christians of
Judæa the break with tradition was terrible,
was almost unthinkable. What was the
consequence ? The Churches of Judæa stood
on one side, the Churches of the world on
the other side. Could they remain one
Church ?

It seems probable that the faith of many
in Judæa broke down under the strain. The
national movement that led to war with Rome
was drawing them ; the crowd of Gentile
converts repelled them. The Remnant once
more shrank. Of the " many myriads " of
Jewish believers mentioned by St. Luke it
is probable that very few went out with the
successor of James when they saw Jerusalem
encompassed by armies. The majority would
seem to have relapsed into Judaism, and to
have shared the fate of their people. The
disruption feared by St. Paul took place, but
it was not a schism among believers ; it was
the falling away of some.

What St. Paul feared, what he saw forming,

what he laboured to destroy, was a wall of division separating believers, and making two distinct Churches. Judæa was over against the world; he tried to obliterate that distinction by mutual works of charity. They of Achaia should minister in carnal things to the poor among "the saints that are at Jerusalem," of whose spiritual things they had been made partakers. The saints at Jerusalem also would make some spiritual gain. "Through the proving of you by this ministration," he wrote to the Church of Corinth, "they glorify God for the obedience of your confession unto the gospel of Christ." There was to be an equality of service rendered. To promote the sense of equality was of paramount importance. The wall of division was not merely geographical; the influence of Judæa spread far; an exclusively Jewish Church, if such a thing could exist, might spring up anywhere in the Diaspora; throughout the world there might be two Churches, and not one.

In the Epistle to the Ephesians, so different in character from St. Paul's other writings, you have a sustained note of triumph over this difficulty. Those who imagine a bitter conflict of Petrine and Pauline Christianity, continuing

after the death of the protagonists, naturally
cannot acknowledge the authenticity of this
Epistle. It is fatal to their theory. But
that dream has faded. I assume the authenticity of the Epistle, and acknowledge its
peculiarity. It is evidently an encyclical. The
occasion which called it forth cannot be
ascertained, but it must have been a great
occasion. Something had happened; something had been done; the wall of partition
was broken down, and the writer hails its
fall with dithyrambic vehemence. Was he
premature? There was that falling away in
Judæa still to be reckoned with. But there
must have been some authoritative decision
going far beyond the compromises which had
never satisfied St. Paul. It was the work of
God in Jesus Christ. "He is our peace, who
made both one, and beat down the middle wall
of partition."

What can we see of the result? Israel is
not forgotten. The Old Testament is not
laid aside. The Church does not become
Gentile. Rather it becomes a larger Israel;
the Remnant is growing to a great multitude.
To achieve this, two things are necessary.
On the one hand, the Gentile Christian must

accept Hebrew origins ; they are made fellow
heirs with the Jews, and the Fathers are
become their fathers. St. Paul treats this as
normal. He tells the Gentile converts, whose
cause has triumphed under his leadership,
that they were formerly "alienated from the
Commonwealth of Israel, and strangers from
the covenants of the promise;" but now they
that were once far off are made nigh with the
Blood of Christ. In this way a tradition was
established which has proved constant. In
the spread of Christendom through the world
few things are more remarkable than the
consent of converted nations to forget their
own people and their fathers' house, their own
origins, and their own heroic age, accepting in
substitution the history and legends, the heroics
and the national memories of the Palestinian
Hebrew. It is not all for good, and there is
a grave question whether the process can be
further extended to the great historic peoples
of Asia. That it has hitherto made for a sense
of unity in Christendom cannot be doubted ;
whether it can be dispensed with the future
must declare. On the other hand, this
surrender of Gentile traditions was balanced
by the complete surrender of the Mosaic Law.

After the first age there is no trace left of a specifically Jewish Christianity. Some features of religion apparently Judaic—a modified sabbatical observance, for example—are of later growth, due to retrospection and the study of the Scriptures of the Old Testament. The Church is the larger Israel, but it is not in the least Jewish.

And yet we abound in definitely Jewish imagery. For us too there is a Jerusalem, the City of our Solemnities. But it is a new Jerusalem. St. Paul struck this note when he declared that Jerusalem above is the Mother of us all. The utter ruin of the Palestinian Jerusalem, and of the polity which it represented, would make this figure the more acceptable ; there is a close connection between that catastrophe and the apocalyptic vision of the Holy City, new Jerusalem, coming down from God out of heaven—" And they shall bring the glory and honour of the nations into it." There is this heavenly Jerusalem, and the Church on earth is conceived as the Diaspora. You find the appropriate word in the Epistle of Clement, addressed by the Church of God sojourning—παροικοῦσα—at Rome to the Church in like condition at

Corinth.   In the same way Polycarp addresses
the Church at Philippi.   The Christian life is
a *peregrinatio*.

Alongside of this Jewish imagery is used
language, equally figurative, drawn from a
Roman source.   When St. Paul was preaching
the Gospel, Roman citizenship was an important factor in human thought.   Himself
born to that franchise, he did not hesitate
to take advantage of it on occasion.   It was
a great distinction, invidious perhaps, but of
practical value.   Two hundred years were yet
to elapse before the edict of Caracalla would
extend the right of citizenship to all the free
inhabitants of the empire, but already vast
numbers of all races and languages were
gathered into its unifying embrace.   You may
be sure that St. Paul had this in mind when he
wrote to the Philippians, the proud possessors
of the rights of a Roman colony, " Our citizenship is in heaven."   What Rome and the
Capitol were to Roman citizens throughout
the empire, that was the Heavenly City to
the people of God scattered abroad in the
world.   This imagery has been less fruitful
than that of Jerusalem, the City of our
Solemnities, but it has not been forgotten ;

you find it repeated precisely in the Epistle to
Diognetus; it has coloured Christian thought,
sometimes in ways that are harmful. The
Church is a civic unit.

One other idea we may gather from St. Paul.
He identified the Lord Jesus with the Seed of
Abraham, but he also went further back.
As there was a first Adam, the progenitor of
the human race, so there is a second Adam,
from whom the faithful derive a new life by
a new birth. Perhaps we owe to this conception
the genealogy of our Lord according to St. Luke,
traced up to Adam, "the son of God." Here
is figured another kind of unity, larger than
that of Israel, larger than any civic unity, but
still unity. As mankind is one, so those
redeemed in Christ out of mankind are one.
There is a real unity in manifold diversity;
unity of spiritual generation, unity of spiritual
constitution, unity of spiritual movement,
unity of thought and conviction. There is
an indestructible unity of mankind, though
we mar it and obscure it by political divisions,
by exaggerated distinctions of race, by prejudice
of education, of habit, and even of colour;
so there is an indestructible unity of Christendom, though marred by self-will and

obscured by inveterate prejudice. There are not two human races ; neither are there two Christian Churches. There is one God, the Father of all men ; one Lord Jesus Christ, incarnate in the common humanity ; one faith in the one Lord ; one hope of our calling, as true sons of Abraham, out of all mankind ; one baptism of the new birth for all the redeemed ; one life-giving Spirit, and one body corporate, formed to be the habitation of the Spirit. The Church is founded in the unity of redeemed mankind.

Unity was achieved in fact by the work of St. Paul. On what does its continuance depend ? What is the nature of the schism that can mar it, or may seem to destroy it ?

E

LECTURE II

THE EPISCOPAL THEORY

Ye are fellow citizens with the saints, and of the household of God, being built upon the foundation of the apostles and prophets, Christ Jesus himself being the chief corner stone.—*Eph.* ii. 29.

WE have to inquire how the unity of the Church is to be maintained, how it is one in much diversity, and how its members are linked together in a social order. It is the purpose of God that we have to ascertain, and, further, the human means by which the end is to be achieved. For the purpose of God demands the ministry of man. It can be hindered and thwarted by human perversity ; it can be achieved only by the operation of divine grace working in human hearts. The prayer of the Lord "that they all may be one" shows this to be an object of search and of endeavour. The prayer "Thy will be done" is not an expression of helpless resignation, but the utterance of a helpful purpose ; the will of God calls us to the task

26

of doing it, and the unity of the faithful which God wills must be sought and maintained by our toil. St. Paul's labours were not superfluous. How are they continued?

There are two ways of conducting this inquiry. You may proceed in the way of high theory, starting from indications of the divine purpose, and deducing thence the necessary forms of human activity. You may proceed by the way of historic method, ascertaining what has been done, and resting in the assurance that the providence of God has directed and controlled the course of events. The weakness of the former method lies in the obscurity of the indications ; the purpose of unity is manifest, but the mode of unity is much less clearly indicated, and there is room for diverse theories. The weakness of the historic method lies in the strain of human perversity ; efforts after unity are not always well directed, and even where successful are not necessarily in accordance with the divine will ; the providence of God overrules the mistakes of men.

There is more safety in a combination of the two methods. It involves an historic study of theory, side by side with a study of

practice. The study of practice will show
where theories fail, and the study of theory
will reduce to order the mere accidents of
practice. I shall make an attempt at this.

A sometime Archbishop of York once used
a striking comparison to illustrate the early
history of the Church. He drew a picture of
a railway train going into a tunnel, and
emerging at the other end with astonishing
modifications ; by careful examination the
observer can satisfactorily identify the train,
but he cannot tell how the modifications were
effected. So for the historical observer the
apostolic Church passes into darkness, and
emerges during the second century, greatly
changed and yet the same. There is some
exaggeration here. The darkness of the
transition is not so complete as it seemed
to us forty years ago. But it is dark. The
light which for a time appeared to be thrown
into it by the discovery of the Didache
has grown dim, and that much bewritten
document has been relegated to an obscurity
of its own. We remain with little information.
The Church of the second century comes into
the light of history with a change great and
unexplained. The apostolate has disappeared.

The change introduces a difficulty. In the writings of St. Paul and in the Acts of the Apostles there is a twofold use of the word *ecclesia* which requires explanation. There is but one Church : that is constantly assumed and is sometimes stated with emphasis. At the same time there are many Churches ; any group of Christians, however small, seems to be called by the same title as the whole body, without any feeling of incongruity. If the word *ecclesia* stands for the unity of the whole people of God, how can it stand also for any fraction of that people ? One thing is clear. The whole is not an aggregate of the parts ; the name is not extended from the particular to the universal : on the contrary, the whole is prior, both logically and in order of time, to the parts which take its name. An explanation of this transference of the name is forthcoming. In any particular group of Christians the whole Church is manifested ; the Church is the Body of Christ, and individual believers are severally members of it ; but Christ is not divided, and therefore the whole Body is present where some of the members are assembled. In one of the two passages of St. Matthew where the Church is mentioned the idea will be found expressed : " Where two or three are gathered together in my Name, there am I in the midst of them."

This seems reasonable. But more is required if these groups are to have any social cohesion. The link is supplied by the apostolate. The Church—not a particular Church, but the universal Church—is built upon the foundation of the apostolate ; it stands in the Apostles' teaching and fellowship —their travels, their visits, their constant supervision, the missions of their delegates, hold the scattered communities together in a social order. And there is more than this. They appoint elders or bishops, officers of familiar style with familiar functions, in the several communities ; we naturally infer that only where such officers are appointed will there be a properly constituted Church, representing the whole Church of God. What we read of St. Paul we may surmise of the other Apostles, with whom he freely compares himself, and we can picture a large activity. All depends upon the Apostles.

Then comes the tunnel. Emerging beyond are found in the second century particular Churches, local Churches, but no Apostles.

Where is the whole Church ? Where is the
link that holds the many in one ?

There are traces of the apostolic method.
As the Apostles wrote epistles to particular
Churches—epistles hortatory, directive, con-
demnatory—so now we find particular Churches
writing epistles to one another. An example
survives in what is known as the First Epistle
of Clement. Addressed by the Church of
God sojourning at Rome to the Church of
God sojourning at Corinth, it treats of factious
disorders which have broken out among the
Christians of that city. This kind of mutual
supervision was probably not unusual. Some
few years later we find St. Ignatius writing to
various Churches epistles of almost apostolic
quality. But Ignatius was not an Apostle : he
was bishop of the particular Church at Antioch.
What sort of authority had he in other
Churches ? What general authority was there
to hold the Church together ?

Look at what Ignatius himself says. He is
anxious about unity, but it is the unity of the
particular Church. Of the nature of this unity
he has a perfectly clear conception. In every
Church he assumes the existence of one bishop,
to whom all the members of the Church are

aggregated.   They are to do nothing without
the bishop ; there are presbyters associated
with him, but they are to him as the strings
to the lyre ; his name and office are indispensable, for a community without bishop and
presbytery cannot be called a Church.[1]

Here is the particular Church of the first
age, with its presbyters or bishops.   But
there is something new.   This one chief, this
necessary centre of unity, is not mentioned
in the apostolic writings.   Whence does he
come ?   That question I shall leave aside.   It is
perhaps insoluble. But however it be answered,
whether you suppose that the bishop of the
second century is the product of a system of
apostolic delegation or that he concentrates
in himself powers that were formerly conferred
on the presbytery at large, you can follow
equally well the argument of the Ignatian
epistles and its consequences.   Neither need
we trouble ourselves to ask whether this kind
of episcopacy was already established everywhere in his day.   He treats it as normal, and
soon afterwards it was universal.

Here, then, is the unity of a particular
Church, the unity of the flock under a single

[1] *Smyrn.* 8 ; *Ephes.* 4 ; *Trall.* 3.   See Appendix I.

pastor. St. Ignatius rates the importance of it very high. He praises the Ephesians for holding it fast, and tells them, " It is good for you to be in blameless unity, that you may always be partakers also of God." But here he stops. In the Ignatian epistles no wider organization is discernible. Anything of the kind on earth seems indeed to be excluded when it is said that Jesus Christ is to the Catholic Church—the first appearance of the phrase in documents known to us—what the bishop is to the particular Church.[1] There is no indication of any means for holding bishops together in unity.

Mutual intercourse like that of the Epistle of Clement seems to be the only bond of union. At the end of the second century you begin to see indications of something more organic. Tertullian's reference to the Churches of special apostolic foundation, where the *cathedrae apostolorum suis locis praesident*,[2] implies a recognition of superior authority residing in the bishops of those places ; the *potentior principalitas* which Irenaeus, in a much debated passage, ascribes to the Church of Rome, appears to be a kind of graded precedence.[3] But there

[1] *Smyrn.* 8.　[2] *De Praescript.* 36.　[3] *Contra Haereses* iii. 3.

F

is nothing definite so far, and in the next
generation you find St. Cyprian formulating
a theory of episcopacy which excludes the
possibility of subordination.

Cyprian's treatise of the unity of the Church
must be read with due regard for its purpose.
He was dealing with perils of faction within
a particular Church, and the direct development of his argument did not carry him
beyond the position of St. Ignatius. The
bishop is the necessary centre of unity in the
local Church. But in seeking a sure basis
for episcopal authority, he found incidentally
a doctrine concerning the relation of bishops
to one another. His argument is not unlike
that which refers the unity of the Church to
the uniqueness of Jesus Christ as the Seed of
Abraham. He refers it to the uniqueness of
the mission of St. Peter, to whom the keys of the
kingdom of heaven are given, and upon whom
the Church is built ; the other Apostles afterwards received exactly the same powers and equal
dignity, but a beginning was made from One for
the purpose of putting emphasis on the real unity
of their commission. The apostolic authority is
therefore denominated *Cathedra Petri*.

This use of the term is almost peculiar to

St. Cyprian. There are obscure indications of
it in Gaul ; in the sixth century you find it
explicit in Gildas ; I do not know where
else to look for examples. You will observe
that it does not mean for St. Cyprian what
cathedrae apostolorum meant for Tertullian. He
probably had in mind that Seat of Moses
on which the Scribes and Pharisees sat as
rulers of Israel.[1] He represents the whole
apostolic company as seated with equal right in
the Chair of Peter, and he passes on at once to
treat the bishops of his own time as their
successors in that place of dignity. Each
several bishop, therefore, occupies the Chair
of Peter, and the unity of the Church depends
on the relation of the faithful to their
appointed pastors. But further, this joint
occupation of the Chair of Peter gives him a
formula for the unity of the episcopate
throughout the whole Church. He uses a
term of Roman Law expressing copartnership :
*Episcopatus unus est, cuius a singulis in solidum
pars tenetur.*[2]

What follows ? In the first place, the
authority of synods. Episcopacy being a

[1] St. Matt. xxiii. 2.
[2] *De Catholicae Ecclesiae Vnitate*, 5. See App. II.

commission of leading and ruling held in common, it is obvious that bishops gathered together in council will have a weightier authority than bishops acting individually. They can act upon each other ; they can make and unmake their colleagues. A candidate should be chosen by the clergy and the faithful, but he is made bishop by the act of other bishops consenting. It is the right and the duty of the faithful to repudiate a bishop who is false to his trust, but he is effectively removed by nothing short of a council of bishops instituting and consecrating his successor.

In the second place there follows an absolute equality of bishops. Cyprian did not merely ignore the precedence of the Apostolic Churches recognized by Tertullian, the *principalitas* of Rome to which Irenaeus testifies ; he definitely rejected the notion of such superiority. Some factious persons at Carthage, condemned by a council of African bishops, appealed to Rome, " ad Petri cathedram adque ad ecclesiam principalem unde unitas sacerdotalis exorta est." These words, which we read in his letter to Cornelius of Rome, are commonly taken to be Cyprian's own, but they are in violent disagreement with what he immediately proceeds to say. He denounces this action of a handful of ruined and desperate men as based on a pretended inferiority of African bishops. His angry protest is incompatible with the recognition of any *principalitas* ; he makes Carthage or indeed any one of the small African Churches, the equal of Rome. I do not think that he could in the same breath use the words quoted. We know, moreover, his opinion about the origin of the *unitas sacerdotalis*, the one united episcopate, and to find the source of it in the Roman Church would be contrary to his express teaching. We know in what sense he spoke of the *Cathedra Petri*, and it would be against his use to place it specifically at Rome. The conclusion seems imperative that he quoted the words in question, not without some touch of scorn, from the " schismatic and profane" letter which the appellants took to Rome for their credentials. For Cyprian himself all Churches, all bishops, were on a footing of absolute equality. Nothing could be superior to a bishop except a synod of bishops.[1]

[1] For the textual basis of the foregoing argument, and of what follows, see Appendix II.

The unity of the Catholic Church stood
in the joint action of bishops, and in the
subordination of each one of them to the
whole college.   And what, then, is schism?
There will be two kinds, which you may
call internal and external.   Internal schism
may be caused in a local Church by a faction
parting company with the bishop, and possibly
setting up a "pseudoepiscopus" against him.
External schism may be caused by a bishop,
or a group of bishops, breaking off relations
of charity with another part of the episcopate.
What degree of unfriendliness would mean
definite rupture is not clear, and Cyprian
probably had no occasion to think out the
question ; he was concerned only with cases
that arose during his short episcopate, and
they were not numerous enough to furnish
even the outline of a system.   His own fierce
quarrel with Stephen of Rome drew from him
no clear statement on this head.

What is the effect of schism ?   You may
take it in two ways.   It is either a division
within the body, or the rending of some
members away from the body.   You have to
take account of both.   Of the former kind
are the schisms and parties which St. Paul

thought to be inevitable in the Corinthian Church ; the latter seems to be indicated where those who will not hear the Church are reduced to the rank of the Gentile and the Publican. St. Cyprian appears to contemplate only this latter effect of schism. The stiffness of his theory of unity caused him to place schismatics altogether outside the Church. He did not distinguish between schism and apostasy. All schismatics, he said roundly, were antichrists. The result is seen in the dispute about baptism. The Church alone, he contended, has the water of life and the power of baptizing ; schismatics have it not ; their pretended baptism is naught, and those who come from them to the Catholic Church must be baptized.[1]

This teaching prepared much trouble for the African Church. Apart from such consequences, St. Cyprian's scheme of unity has obvious weaknesses. It furnishes unlimited opportunity for external schism. The tendency to such division is illustrated by his own experience. Bishops, sharing the episcopate with equal right, would go their own way ; a group of bishops would be superior to any

[1] Ep. lxviiii. 3 ; lxx. 2.

one bishop, and could correct him or remove
him ; but if one group differed from another
group there would be no remedy. The scheme
is therefore incomplete, and that is a grave
fault in a plan so exact and symmetrical. But
there is a worse flaw. The scheme is not in
accordance with facts. Cyprian might protest,
but it was none the less true that the Church
of Rome had a weightier authority than any
Church in Africa ; the Carthaginian schismatics
who appeared *ad ecclesiam principalem* were
keeping fairly close to the line of Christian
tradition. The doctrine of the absolute equality
of bishops was not in agreement with the
practice of the Church. The greatness of the
greater sees was a reality. Their importance
was inevitable, Carthage itself being witness.
St. Cyprian could not help leading his African
colleagues, and it was not his personality alone
that dominated them ; the Church of Carthage,
distracted and turbulent as it was, secured for
its chief a superiority unquestioned.

Irenaeus and Tertullian referred to Churches
of apostolic foundation, the Roman Church
above all, as the surest depositories of the
Christian tradition. Precedence, however, was
not determined exclusively by this consideration.

Otherwise, Alexandria could hardly have taken the second place, Corinth would have had a rank to which it never pretended, Carthage would have had no eminence, and the Church of Milan would not have won the distinction attaching to it even before it was illustrated by the genius and the sanctity of Ambrose. The elevation of Constantinople is but the crowning example of a process by which other Churches had been lifted to a position of superior dignity and authority. It is impossible to identify any one exclusive cause of such distinction. When the Fathers of Chalcedon declared that Rome had been given the first place in the Church because it was the Imperial City, their history was probably at fault, but they bore witness to a current opinion of what was reasonable, and they found in this a justification of the rank now accorded to the New Rome. An organization of the universal episcopate on these lines was become possible. The political divisions of the Roman Empire were found serviceable ; in place of indeterminate groups, we find the bishops of each province assembled in regular synods, and the bishop of the metropolitan city is their permanent president ; equality is at an end

G

when they are not allowed to act without
him, and when his consent is required for
their appointment. We must not seek the
origin of these rules in formal legislation ; the
decrees of councils on the subject rather fix
the practice than create it ; an obvious need
has produced it, and its form is determined
by an equally obvious convenience. Grouping
proceeds to a further stage when the Second
General Council at Constantinople has made
rules concerning the action of the greater sees,
which point the way to the future development
of the Patriarchate.

These arrangements, however, did not
become universal. We are not to think of
them as final, or as fixing the normal constitution of the episcopate. The Patriarchal
system did not cover the whole Church ; to
the west of Rome it had no meaning. Not
even the metropolitical system took firm root
there until it received a new form under
metropolitans endowed with special powers by
delegation from the Roman Pontiff. We see
a more spontaneous growth taking the form
of national episcopates. Political demarcation
was used here as in the East, though with
less precision, the kingdoms carved out of

the Roman Empire providing a framework. The great series of Spanish councils affords the best example. The capitularies of Frankish kings, on their ecclesiastical side, are records of similar proceedings. I reserve the papacy for separate treatment, but I note that even a system rather imperial than national did not entirely destroy this tendency to nationalism, which became strong in proportion as the central power grew weak. When the fortunes of the papacy were at their lowest ebb the Council of Constance was organized by Nations, and the arrangement seemed to have a promise of permanence; the reviving influence of Rome speedily destroyed it, but Lyndwood—himself the most pronounced of papists—could still say that the *ecclesia anglicana*, though canonically no more than two separate provinces, was in effect an incorporated unit, *quaedam universitas*.[1] The disputes about the Pragmatic Sanction of Bourges showed the French bishops inclined to make even larger claims, and the Concordat of 1516 opened the way to the assertion of the Gallican Liberties. Febronianism might have made as great a stir in the eighteenth century if the prince-bishops

[1] *Provinciale*, Lib. iii. tit. 28.   Edit. 1679, p. 266.

of Germany had been less obviously unfitted
for the part of spiritual leaders. Looking back
again, you will note some national episcopates
surviving the general revolt against the papacy
which we call the Reformation. It may seem
to be the last word in paradox to adduce
Scottish Presbyterianism as an example, but
I shall have occasion to show that it is not
altogether absurd. In our own day we see
similar developments in the East, a curious
effect of Turkish rule ; not only are severed
Churches like the Armenian and the Bulgarian
so organized, but others also in communion
with the Orthodox Patriarchs have episcopates
ordered on strict lines of political nationality,
and there are Uniats under the papacy in
similar case.

These facts, thus briefly recalled, show that
an episcopal theory of the Church is not tied to
the rigid scheme of St. Cyprian, nor even to the
modification of it brought about by the metropolitical system. It is seen to allow more
flexibility than has commonly been recognized.
Reduced to essentials, it includes only these
three elements : the relation of the pastor and
the flock, the institution of a college of pastors,
and the maintenance of unity—I borrow

St. Cyprian's phrase—by the conglutination of bishops.

Is it adequate? Does it give a sufficient account of the unity of the Church?

It fails in face of external schism. Bishops are human. The *gluten* of charity will not always hold them together. You may organize their college in such sort that individual aberrations will be reduced to order; the authority of a synod will suffice to hold a provincial group together, or, in the last resort, to remove a recalcitrant member; but, however articulate the organization may be, whole groups will be able to fly apart. Ecclesiastical history is full of such schisms, which can be healed only by patience, and which easily become inveterate. Those who take their stand upon the episcopal theory are driven to the subterfuge of disregarding these divisions. You may persuade yourself to be content with a branch theory which seeks the one Body of Christ in three or four different hierarchies, standing to each other, at the best, in a relation of polite aloofness. But it is not really satisfactory.

Equal failure is possible in face of internal schism. You may be able to dispose of the

claims put forward by schismatics who acknowledge no bishop ; you may settle the case of
one intruding bishop, whose condemnation by
a provincial synod will save the unity of the
Church in the sense that he will no longer
trouble its peace from within ; but what if
there be a whole provincial group of dissidents,
hierarchy rivalling hierarchy in the same field ?
If you stand on the episcopate one may be
as good as another. You will easily fit this
question to well-known local conditions. If
you try to determine in favour of one or the
other hierarchy you must either measure them
by a standard apart from episcopacy or form
an arbitrary judgement which you will hardly
reckon tolerable. To find intolerable judgements of this sort, you have only to look
through William Palmer's *Treatise of the Church*.
Here in America these problems press upon
you. I think you will not be satisfied with
a systematic theory which fastens upon your
Russian neighbours of New York the guilt of
schism or alternatively retorts the same charge
upon yourselves. You will say that there
must be something wrong with the theory.

Indeed, there is an obvious fault. It puts
too much upon episcopacy. How can you

make an *articulus stantis aut cadentis ecclesiae*
of that which did not exist in the first age of
the Church ?   How can that be the one bond
of unity, the lack of which did not prevent
the Church from being one and united in
the day of St. Paul ?   You may insist on the
necessity of the apostolic foundation ; you
may demand the continuity of the apostolic
fellowship ; you cannot require, for the fulfilment of either condition, an organization of
the Church to which the Apostles themselves
were strangers.   On the high ground of theory
you must allow that any effective way of
maintaining apostolic unity will suffice ; on
the broad ground of history you must observe
that the way in use, the episcopal way, has
been subject to modification.   You must
assume an apostolic origin for the institution
of episcopacy, for no other account of it seems
possible ; but there is nothing to show that
the Apostles made it irrevocably the one and
only safeguard of unity.   Neither Ignatius nor
Cyprian seems to be acquainted with any such
tradition ; they took episcopacy as a fact of
experience, and you must be content to do
the same.   It was an instrument of unity ; if
you try to make it the only possible instrument,

fixed and indispensable, you will put more upon it than the tradition warrants.

Another consideration points the same way. An old difficulty recurs. *Quis custodiet ipsos custodes?* The bishops are the appointed guardians of unity. If they are faithless— and the state of Christendom shows that they have not been wholly faithful—who shall bring them to reason? You will say that the Holy Spirit works in them and with them, countering their faults, nullifying their mistakes, making good their defects. You can hardly say anything better. So you hope for restored unity. But now you have shifted your ground. You no longer depend on the conglutination of bishops for the bond of unity; you depend on the working of the Spirit. You cannot limit that working. Episcopacy has been the instrument of the Spirit, but it is a flexible instrument, moulded to the needs of successive times; it is conceivable that it may be changed out of recognition or that another instrument may be found. You may hold with unhesitating faith that the Church of Christ is one, and that its unity will in good time be made manifest, but it may be unwise to pin your faith exclusively to episcopacy.

LECTURE III

THE PAPAL THEORY

Simon, Simon, behold Satan asked to have you, that he might sift you as wheat : but I made supplication for thee, that thy faith fail not : and do thou, when once thou hast turned again, stablish thy brethren.—*St. Luke* xxii. 31.

" SERVUS servorum Dei : " from the time of St. Gregory the Great it has been the proudest title of the Roman Pontiff. "Whosoever would become great among you shall be your servant ; and whosoever would be first among you shall be your bondsman : even as the Son of Man came not to be ministered unto, but to minister." That is the evangelic law of precedence, borne in mind through all aberrations of worldly ambition. Popes may have acted as lords over God's heritage, but they have based their claim on this title ; they take the curse of Ham, and construe it into a blessing. Bishops and priests are appointed to minister, servants of

49   H

God and of God's people ; the Pope is the servant of servants.

The title has not been borne in vain. There are many dark days in the history of the papacy, days of intolerable shame as well as days of disaster, but the record in the main is good. The Popes have been set to maintain the unity of the Church ; they claim this for their calling ; if they have failed, it is not for want of labour. At times, you may think, their work has been rather divisive than unifying, but that you may put down to very human mistakes ; you must allow, if you make a candid study of history, that the papacy has been an instrument of the Spirit for maintaining the unity of the Body ; you can hardly doubt that it is still being used in that sense. But more is claimed for it. It is said to be a necessary instrument, necessary by a sort of natural necessity according to the will of God ; the one Body must have one head visible here on earth. It is said to be an unfailing instrument ; the true Church consists only of those who are linked in visible unity with this one head ; those who are severed from the head are severed from the Body, which remains in itself whole and undivided. You see the

resemblance of this scheme of unity to that
of St. Cyprian ; the Roman Pontiff is substituted
for the general episcopate, the rest is the same.
There is a papal theory of unity.

Let us go straight to the most authentic
statement of it. You will find this in the
Constitution *Pastor Aeternus* of the Vatican
Council.[1] It is there laid down that the unity
of the Church, according to the prayer of our
Lord on the night of his betrayal, is for all
time secured by the selection of Peter as the
principle of unity and the visible foundation
upon which all stands, by the grant of a true
and proper jurisdiction over the other Apostles
to Peter in person, and by the continuance
of this jurisdiction over the whole Church
in the Roman Pontiff as holding the same
special office in perpetual succession. These
are the three essentials. Peter is not only
the starting-point of unity, as St. Cyprian
taught ; the other Apostles were added to
him, not as equal holders of exactly the same
commission, but as subordinates ; and he has
one particular successor, to whom the bishops
and pastors of the Church, as successors to
the apostolate in general, are in like manner

[1] See Appendix IV.

subordinate.   So far it is a perfectly clear and
consistent theory.

I must add one detail.   The continuance of
the apostolate is implied.   The Roman Pontiff
is not the successor of Peter in the sense in
which bishops are successors of the Apostles,
exercising the same pastoral office in a different
manner and under different conditions ; he
executes the office of Peter in the same manner
and under the same conditions.   According to
the episcopal theory which I was considering in
my last lecture, the great difference between
Apostle and bishop is that the one has a general
mission to the whole world, while the other
has a particular mission locally circumscribed ;
collectively the bishops rule the whole Church,
as the Apostles did, but individually they have
a limited charge.   So the episcopate, though
succeeding to the function of the apostolate,
is not identified with the apostolate ; we can
say that the apostolate disappeared, and was
replaced by the episcopate.   But in the papal
theory which we are now considering, there
is no such distinction.   The Roman Pontiff
is Peter ; the cry of the assembled Fathers at
Chalcedon, "Peter has spoken by Leo," is
a plain statement of fact, and no mere

rhetorical flourish ; Peter himself, says the Vatican Council, lives and presides and gives judgement in his successors, the bishops of the holy Roman See.[1] The *cathedra Petri* is at Rome ; the appellants against the judgement of Cyprian were right. This, and nothing less, is the *potentior principalitas* of the Roman Church.

The Council says that this power of the Roman Pontiff is *uere episcopalis*. The purport of the statement is not clear. It might be directed against those who contend that the papacy is to be distinguished from the bishopric of Rome, that the Roman Pontiff holds two distinct offices which might even be separated, one in which he stands like other bishops in succession to the Apostles, the other in which he succeeds to the special prerogatives of Peter. But the context points to another meaning. The "truly episcopal" jurisdiction of the Roman Pontiff is said to be "immediate," extending alike to all pastors and to all the faithful throughout the whole Church. The

[1] The words are evidently taken from the address of Philip, legate of the Apostolic See to the Council of Ephesus, confirming what had been done in the Council before his arrival : ὅστις ἕως τοῦ νῦν καὶ ἀεὶ ἐν τοῖς διαδόχοις καὶ ζῇ καὶ δικάζει.—*Actio* iii, Mansi, iv. 1295.

statement seems, therefore, to be directed against those who assert for the papacy a merely appellant jurisdiction, an authority for controlling other bishops, and mediately through them directing the life of the Church. The Council explicitly condemns those who attribute to the Pope only "an office of inspection or direction." His claim is that every Christian man is immediately subject to his ordinary jurisdiction, as well as to the ordinary jurisdiction of the diocesan bishop. In this sense, it would seem, his authority is "uere episcopalis." It is not easily to be distinguished from that which St. Gregory the Great supposed to be assumed by John the Faster, when he denounced the Patriarch's purpose of subjugating to himself, as "uniuersus episcopus," all the members of Christ.[1]   One is reminded of a famous saying to which a new turn may be given.   St. Ignatius compares the relation of a bishop to his flock with the relation of Jesus Christ to the whole Church, making our Lord the universal Bishop.   " Where the bishop is," he says, " there let the people be, even as where Christ Jesus is, there is the Catholic Church." [2] The Vatican Council would say, " Where the

[1] *Ep.* v. 47.   [2] *Smyrn.* 8.

Roman Pontiff is, there is the Catholic
Church."

This gives us the principle of unity in the
Church according to the papal theory. As is
the bishop to his particular flock, so is the Pope
to the whole people of God. All the teaching
of Ignatius and Cyprian about the bishop as
the organ of unity may be transferred to him.
The Vatican Council is explicit : these things
are so ordered " that by the maintenance of
unity, alike of communion and of belief, with
the Roman Pontiff, the Church of Christ may
be one flock under one chief shepherd." And
this unity is maintained by the exercise of
jurisdiction. That is implied in the teaching
of the Vatican Council ; it is clearly stated in
the encyclical *Satis cognitum* of Leo XIII, which
may be taken as a commentary on the Council.
" It is for Peter," you will there read, " to
uphold the Church and to keep it firmly bound
together by unbreakable links. But who
could fulfil such a task without that power
of commanding, of forbidding, and of judging
which is truly and appropriately called jurisdiction ? States and commonwealths surely stand
by nothing but the power of jurisdiction. A
chieftainship of honour, and that thin function

of counsel and advice which is called 'direction,'
cannot bring to any human society the boon
either of unity or of strength." Very significant
is this fearless comparison of the Church with
a civil commonwealth.   Unity means the same
in both cases ; it is unity of jurisdiction.
The unity of the Church is the unity of a
jurisdiction exercised exclusively by the Roman
Pontiff as representing St. Peter.   It is, no
doubt, much more than this, something more
intimately religious ; but all else depends on
this.   The papacy is the organ of unity ; the
way of unity for Christian men is the way of
religious subjection to the jurisdiction of the
Roman Pontiff.

    And what is schism according to this theory ?
I will ask you to recall the convenient distinction that I have drawn between internal and
external schism.   According to the episcopal
theory internal schism is faction within a
particular Church, which may extend to the
setting up of a rival bishop against the lawful
occupant of the see ; external schism is a breach
of intercommunion between divers bishops.
But now we have to do with a single episcopal
or apostolic authority extending over the whole
world.   External schism will therefore have no

meaning, for nothing is external. When Gregory VII lay dying he bemoaned himself : " I have loved righteousness and hated iniquity, therefore I die in exile." A monk who waited on him replied : " In exile thou canst not be, my lord, for God hath given thee the heathen for thine inheritance, and the utmost part of the earth for thy possession." It was finely said. The papal claim has never been more nobly expressed. You see what it means : the whole world is one pastoral charge. There is no question of bishops being in communion with each other ; every one of them is either in communion with the Roman Pontiff or not in communion with him ; those in communion with him are as a matter of course in communion with each other, and that is the only kind of intercommunion that counts.

All schism is therefore brought into the category of internal schism. There is one Chief Pastor, and schism is a factious refusal of the obedience due to him. Bishops, or groups of bishops, may refuse it ; they are schismatics. Their people may follow them in disobedience ; they also are schismatics. Individuals or whole communities may break away from bishops who submit to the Pope's

I

authority; they are schismatics. On the other hand, to break away from a bishop who is himself not in communion with the Pope is certainly no act of schism, and may be a return to the way of unity.

So far, all is plain sailing. But now we come to a difficulty. There are the antipopes. If the extreme development of schism within a particular Church is reached with the promotion of a rival bishop to challenge the lawful occupant of the see, there will be a like development within the universal Church when a rival Pope is raised up to contest the occupancy of the Chair of St. Peter. It has often been done; from the second century to the fifteenth, antipopes are numerous. And how shall it be known which of the two claimants—or three, it may be—is the true successor of St. Peter? When two rival bishops claim an ordinary see, some authority may be found to arbitrate between them: a council of bishops, or perhaps the Roman Pontiff. It is allowed that such an authority is superior to an individual bishop, may judge him, and even depose him; it can certainly, therefore, determine the question whether he is a true bishop or *pseudo-episcopus*. But when the papacy itself is in dispute, who shall decide? It is a maxim of the papal theory that the Pope judges all, and is judged of none. The Roman Pontiff, says Leo XIII, has all parts of Christendom, "etiam una collectas," subject to him. An ecumenical council, comprising every other bishop in the world, and speaking unanimously, would still be his inferior. To what judgement shall one who claims to be the Roman Pontiff submit his claim? When there are two claimants, they will mutually condemn each other, and there is no appeal.

What are the effects of such schism? Is the Church divided, or are the schismatics cast out? This question is not determined by the Vatican Council. I turn again to the encyclical of Leo XIII. He also avoids—whether of set purpose or no may be doubted—any express solution. But there are two phrases which in their context seem to be determinative; a condemned heretic is "ab ecclesia extorris," an exile from the Church; those who are not in communion with the unity of the Church—he quotes from St. Augustine—"non sunt in Ecclesia." I will not cite anything that is merely a theological inference; the most official teaching about the papal theory puts

forward the Cyprianic doctrine that the true
Church is in fact indivisible, and that schism
is definite separation from the Church. It
is taught with sufficient clearness. But not
with the rigour, the African hardness, of
St. Cyprian. I shall not concern myself here
with the language commonly used about those
who are " of the soul of the Church," though
not of the body. That belongs to another
order of ideas. We are considering the
unity of the body. The exclusion of schismatics even from the body of the Church is
subject to modification. I draw three illustra-
tions from the public practice of the Roman
Church.

This first. In contrast with the vehement
assertions of St. Cyprian, we find the validity
of sacraments administered by schismatics to
be completely acknowledged, with partial exceptions only in respect of marriage and the sacrament of penance. This difference dates from
St. Cyprian's own day, for his serious quarrel
with the Roman Church arose out of diverging
practice in regard to baptism administered by
heretics or schismatics. It will hardly be contended that sacramental ministrations are not
activities of the Body of Christ, which are thus

made to extend beyond the supposed unity of the Church.

In the second place, I observe a limit set to the effect of excommunication. A person excommunicate is obviously not in communion with the Roman Pontiff, and is therefore *ex hypothesi* not " in the Church." Yet an excommunicate cardinal is allowed to take part in the election of a pope.[1] For this purpose, then, he is allowed to act as if within the Church.

My third illustration I draw from the present rules of the Roman Church about the celebration of marriage. They have been much discussed, more hotly than wisely, and some of their implications have been overlooked. The Church has claimed an effective control of the contract of marriage made between Christians, and power to invalidate the contract where canonical requirements are ignored. But the Church has never claimed jurisdiction over those who are not Christians, and their marriages are left to the law of nature, or to the laws of the civil community in which they live. Until recently the rules of the Church in this matter were treated as extending theoretically to all

[1] Lucius Lector, *Le Conclave*, pp. 98, 120, 131.

persons baptized, whether in communion with
the Church or not ; the decrees of the Council
of Trent, for reasons of practical convenience,
were not imposed in some regions, but they
were imposed, if at all, on all the baptized alike.
Here is a claim to hold baptized heretics and
schismatics within the compass of the Church.
But the decree *Ne temere* of 1907 made a change.
The baptized are now distinguished as *catholici*
or *acatholici*. To those who are *acatholici* this
new legislation does not apply. Here, then,
the principle of the exclusion of schismatics
from the Church seems to be upheld. But
only to be modified. For the effect of the
decree extends to " all who have been baptized
in the Catholic Church and all who have been
converted to it from heresy or schism, even
though they may afterwards have broken away
from the same." [1]   Those who have once been
within the unity of the Church are not removed
by subsequent schism from the jurisdiction of
the Church. It appears, therefore, that they
are not thrust entirely outside.

[1] *Ne temere*, xi. 1 : Statutis superius legibus tenentur
omnes in catholica Ecclesia baptizati et ad eam ex haeresi
aut schismate conuersi, licet siue hi siue illi ab eadam postea
defecerint.

There is clearly, then, some uncertainty in the treatment of schism. But schism and unity are correlative, and a weakness in one part of the system infects the whole. Either the papal theory of unity is not quite consistent with itself, or the practice is not quite consistent with the theory. Perhaps the theory has not yet been worked out to all its logical consequences. It is not pretended that the papacy has always been the same in action. It has developed. It has sometimes been a very feeble institution. It has risen, and sunk, and risen again. The utmost that is claimed for it is that in principle it has always been there. Its fortunes can be traced in history.

Taken by themselves, the Petrine texts are not a very sure standing-ground. They are patient of more than one interpretation. They do not expressly indicate any successor to the prerogatives of St. Peter, whatever those prerogatives may have been. The Cyprianic theory of episcopacy was equally built on these texts, making all the Apostles and all bishops alike inheritors of all the functions first assigned to Peter. It must, however, be observed that the charge, " Stablish thy brethren," especially when the time and the circumstances are con-

sidered, suggests a commission which was not
to be shared with the rest ; and this seems to
me a much surer starting-point for the papal
theory than the name of the Rock or the
singular gift of the Keys. Yet even here
there is no hint of succession, and succession,
if assumed, might be otherwise understood.
It is open to any rigid Cyprianist to argue that
the charge has been passed on to all bishops,
who in the fervour of conversion are mutually
to stablish one another. It is not upon the
Petrine texts that the papal theory stands, but
upon an interpretation of the texts.

You search history for that interpretation.
You find from very early times a great dignity,
a great authority, attached to the Roman Church.
There is a *principalitas* ; and this, whatever it
may mean, is connected with the *Cathedra Petri*,
established at Rome and understood in a sense
unlike that of St. Cyprian. Cyprian's own
protest is evidence for the fact. Here you
seem to have the papacy in germ. But, on the
other hand, you may have here only the most
conspicuous example of that preference for
Churches of apostolic foundation which Tertullian evinces, or of that inevitable leadership
of the greater Churches which created the

patriarchates. A Greek theologian will probably say that all the evidence points to this,
and to nothing more.

But something more there was. You find
it before the end of the second century in the
treatment of the Quartodecimans ; you find it
soon afterwards in the baptismal controversy.
Victor and Stephen, Bishops of Rome, assume
an authority which is more than episcopal, and
not less than apostolic. The assumption is
denounced by some who are opposed to them,
and perhaps deprecated by some who agree
with them, but there seems to be no reason for
doubting that it was a tradition of their own
Church. This special authority of the Roman
bishop was " felt, rather than defined," says
Duchesne ;[1] there was a feeling of it at Rome,
and the rest of the Church was more or less
conscious of it. There are some curious
variants. St. Gregory the Great, who did not
fail on occasion to assert the dignity of his see,
once wrote of this Petrine *principatus* as shared

---

[1] *Hist. ancienne de l'Eglise*, i. 536 : Celle-ci était plus
sentie que définie ; sentie d'abord par les Romains eux-
mêmes, qui, depuis saint Clément, n'hésitèrent jamais sur
leurs devoirs envers l'ensemble de la chrétienté ; sentie aussi
par les autres, pour autant que cette impression n'était pas
contrariée par quelque préoccupation de circonstance.

K

equally by Alexandria and Antioch.[1] But the
claim for Rome in particular was more general.
The claim was allowed or disputed as circumstances required. It was continuously put
forward, and it continuously found support
from one part or another of the Christian
Church. The papacy of to-day has grown,
with no violently new departures, out of the
practice of the Roman Church to intervene
more or less beneficially in the affairs of other
Churches. You may trace back that practice,
if you will, to the Epistle of Clement. It is
no unreasonable assumption to base it upon
a privilege assigned to St. Peter. That is the
strength of the papal theory. That, and its
appeal as a peculiarly practical guarantee of
unity. It demands examination from both
points of view.

You will not expect me to enter on this examination. Long rows of controversial volumes
forbid a brief survey. This only I will say of

[1] *Ep.* vii. 40 : Cum multi sint apostoli, pro ipso tamen
principatu sola apostolorum principis sedes in auctoritate
conualuit quae in tribus locis unius est. . . . Cum ergo
unius atque una sit sedes, cui ex auctoritate diuina tres
nunc episcopi praesident, quicquid ego de uobis boni audio,
mihi imputo, si quid de me boni creditis hoc uestris
meritis impertate. The latter is addressed to Eulogius of
Alexandria.

the historic question, that the very existence of a case against the papal theory endangers its stability. The case for the episcopate, as inheriting some functions of the apostolate, is overwhelmingly strong ; if the papacy were an office derived immediately from Peter, you would expect the case for it to be at least equally well supported, the unanimity of the Church to be equally clear from the first. It is not so. Candid supporters of the papal theory, historians like Duchesne and Funk, find the institution, as I have said, only in germ during the formative period. In the fourth century, says Duchesne, there was no central authority recognized and active ; the papacy of later ages was yet to be born.[1] But on the other hand a germinal principle, if real, is not to be treated as nothing.

For my own part, I think the papal theory is more likely to break down under its own weight than to break up under the blows of historic criticism. So much is made to depend on so little. Such intolerable consequences follow. The Church is narrowed to a sect. There is something obviously wrong when the

[1] Duchesne, *op. cit*, ii. 660 ; Funk, *Lehrbuch der Kirchenge-schichte*, pp. 164–66.

whole Catholic Church of Christ is made to include only a minority of Christians—of those who are freely acknowledged to be Christians. A minority, and even a small minority, may have a monopoly of the truth; against a world groaning to find itself Arian, Athanasius may stand secure; but if the division becomes permanent you will begin to doubt the sufficiency of the minority. When you see the orthodox East, hierarchies and believers who possess unchallenged the whole range of sacramental grace, almost entirely excluded from the ambit of the Catholic Church, you are compelled to ask whether a theory that excludes them can possibly be sound.

But even as applied to the narrowed limits of its own making, the papal theory develops grave weaknesses. It promises security against heresy and schism; it achieves security in neither field.

There is no security against heresy. The Pope can bind error upon the Church. His jurisdiction, suffering no control and no appeal, may be used for the protection of heretics or for the expulsion of the orthodox. All is made to depend upon one man. He is human. The doctrine of his infallibility, if

it be true, is no safeguard, for it is not
pretended that he is invariably infallible.
He is held to be protected from error, by
the divine assistance, only when he is defining
ex cathedra some doctrine concerning faith or
morals to be held by the universal Church.
That can rarely be done ; but the papal
jurisdiction is constantly at work for good or
for evil, and there is no promise of infallibility
in its exercise. That jurisdiction, which
Leo XIII has declared to be the indispensable
organ of unity, may hold the Church united
either in truth or in error. St. Gregory the
Great saw this peril when he was objecting to
the title of Universal Bishop assumed by John
the Faster. He constantly repeated the
argument that, if one bishop be called
universal, the universal Church crumbles
into ruin with his fall.[1] That dispute was
about a title ; the Easterns may have been
right in thinking that Gregory made much
ado about nothing, and in delicately hinting
that he misunderstood the Greek word used ;

---

[1] *Ep.* vii. 27 : Si unus episcopus uocatur uniuersalis uniuersa ecclesia corruit si unus uniuersus cadit. v. 43 : Cum
fortasse in errore perit qui uniuersus dicitur, nullus iam
episcopus remansisse in statu ueritatis inuenitur.

but he took it to imply effective jurisdiction over the whole Church, and in the hands of one man, he said, this might prove fatal.

And there is no security against schism. How many antipopes have there been? From Callixtus and Hippolytus to Eugenius and Felix, from the third century to the fifteenth, I reckon not less than thirty-six. You must remember that in every case the papal theory provides no authority for adjudicating between the rival claimants. St. Cyprian and his African colleagues could examine the records of election and decide whether they would recognize Cornelius or Novatian as the true Bishop of Rome;[1] but according to this theory they had no authority so to act, and if their decision had been wrong,

---

[1] Cypr. *Epp.* xliiii, xlviii. It is curious that Leo XIII, in the encyclical *Satis cognitum*, should have quoted St. Cyprian's words, "Communicare cum Cornelio, hoc est cum catholica ecclesia communicare" (*Ep.* lv, slightly altered), as implying that communion with Rome is a test of Catholicity. The question of the moment was not whether Antonianus, to whom he was writing, was in communion with the Roman Church, but whether he communicated with the party of Cornelius or with that of Novatian as the true Catholic Church at Rome. Cp. *Ep.* xlviii : "Communicationem tuam, id est catholicae ecclesiae unitatem."

they would merely have shut themselves out from the Catholic Church. Consider the state of things at the end of the Great Schism. Three rivals claim the Chair of St. Peter ; the Churches of France and of England formally withdraw their obedience from this one or that, or from all alike ; the question whether their action is schismatical or not depends on a previous question, insoluble in principle, as to the rights of the several claimants ; [1] the Council of Constance settles the conflict by a prudent evasion, compelling or persuading all three to resign, and charging the three Colleges ot Cardinals—two of which must *ex hypothesi* be schismatical — to make a common election. What a coil ! And what is to prevent a recurrence of the trouble ? I must once more quote St. Gregory the Great on the title of Universal Bishop : " Ecce ex hoc nefando elationis uocabulo ecclesia scinditur." [2]

[1] I do not forget the arguments by which Franzelin (*Theses de Ecclesia Christi*, pp. 230–38) and others have attempted to prove that Urban VI and his immediate successors to Gregory XII were indisputably the true Pontiffs. They seem to me very weak. How can we ignore the statement of the Cardinals themselves that they had not canonically elected Urban ?

[2] *Ep.* v. 44.

The usual answer is that the providence of God must be relied upon to prevent or to heal such schism. A pious conclusion, but a confession of the bankruptcy of the theory. The unity of the Church no longer depends on the papacy ; it depends on the providence of God. The papal jurisdiction is no longer the one essential and indestructible organ of unity. It is, at most, an instrument in the hand of God, which may break ; and when it breaks another instrument must be found. It may be a Council, as at Constance, or it may be what the wisdom of God shall choose.

There can be no difficulty about acknowledging the papacy as a provisional instrument. There need be no difficulty about acknowledging the Petrine dignity of the Holy See. For the best of the Popes—indeed for most of them—it may fairly be said that they have acted on the charge, "when thou hast turned again, stablish thy brethren." But it is a long way from that to the acceptance of the papal theory as true. Is the papal jurisdiction a guarantee of unity ? Look round upon Christendom. It may hold together those who accept it without question. But that is sectarian unity, the unity of those who agree in a particular opinion. Is that the unity of the whole Church of Christ? The papacy has done great things, but there is one thing that it has not done; it has not held all Christians together. It has not held even the majority of them together. It has claimed too much. It has attempted more than could be done by the means employed. We must look elsewhere for the unity of the Church.

L

LECTURE IV

THE SECTARIAN CONCEPTION

The servants say unto him, Wilt thou then that we go and gather them up? But he saith, Nay; lest haply while ye gather up the tares, ye root up the wheat with them.—*St. Matt.* xiii. 28.

I HAVE spoken of a kind of unity which is sectarian. My purpose to-day is to examine this and to contrast it with the wider unity of the Church of Christ.

What is a sect? It is a group of men who are associated either as followers of a leader or as upholders of a doctrine. The former idea has given us the word, but we use it more frequently in the latter sense. A sect is not necessarily an evil thing. It is legitimate, and, perhaps, even useful, in the form of a political party. But we deprecate party spirit, and we have no good word for sectarianism. There is, therefore, an abuse of sect, and we seldom use the word except in this connection. Sectarianism has no defenders; we accuse

74

one another of it, and we labour all alike to rebut the accusation.

It is obvious that the Christian Church may be called, in the strict sense of the word, a sect. We are followers of a Master, and we are distinguished from the rest of mankind by so doing. We stand for a certain doctrine of God, and so again we are distinguished. It is equally obvious that there can be sects within the Christian Church. There were some at Corinth who said they were "of Paul," or "of Apollos," or "of Cephas," and St. Paul rebuked them as sectaries ; it is not clear from his account whether there were others who said in the same sectarian temper that they were "of Christ," but we are familiar in our own day with those who in this sense call themselves "Christians." It is clear also that these were not merely harmless parties within the Church. They ran the risk of breaking up the unity of the Church. The Apostle asked with indignation, "Is Christ divided?" But, on the other hand, it is clear that you can have within the Church sects, of a kind similarly named, which will be harmless ; the Order of St. Benedict and the Order of St. Francis do not threaten

disruption. But yet again, where disruption
is imminent or actual, it is still possible to
speak of a sect without implication of blame.
When dealing with Donatism, Constantine
could write without offence, and probably
under the most orthodox direction, of the
" Catholic sect." [1] But the meaning of the
word has hardened, and with us it always
implies a hostile judgement.

There is a reason for this limitation of the
term. The Church of Christ is catholic,
universal, not only in the way of extension,
but also in point of doctrine ; its function
is to teach what St. Paul claimed to have
taught at Ephesus, " the whole counsel of
God." You will not take that to mean an
encyclopaedic system of theology, but you
will understand that the Apostle wilfully
obscured nothing, and that he tried to keep
all truths correlated in a true proportion.
According to a memorable phrase, to be
Catholic is to observe the proportion of faith.
To be sectarian is to be out of proportion,
to insist unduly on some things, with a

[1] Eusebius, *H.E.* x. 5, Imperial Letter to Chrestus of
Syracuse : τῆς αἱρέσεως τῆς καθολικῆς. The Latin original
probably had the word *secta*.

consequent neglect of other things. *Secta* is originally the Latin equivalent of αἵρεσις. The derivatives of the two words differ only in usage ; fundamentally they have the same meaning ; for our day the words *sect* and *heresy* alike have lost their innocence, and are used only of that which is accounted evil.

I may seem to be going a long way about to arrive at what is obvious, but it is well to put the meaning of our terms beyond the possibility of mistake. I am looking for something that may help us in our study of unity and schism. And I note this first ; that sectarian unity is a much simpler thing than Catholic unity, since it stands on a basis usually very narrow, and never to be compared with the rich complex of Catholic faith and practice. And this in the second place ; that a sect is not necessarily schismatic, however much it may incline to schism, and conversely that schism is not necessarily sectarian. I would find out what is the sectarian conception of unity, and what kind of schism is the outcome of it.

Two characteristic schisms, sufficiently remote to be studied with detachment, will afford a starting-point. Novatianism and Donatism had something in common, though they ran

very different courses. Both sprang from a
puritan conception of the Church. A certain
standard was set, a particular standard to which
the Church must conform. The Church is
holy, and a lapse from holiness is a falling away
from that essential quality ; moral defects mean
apostasy. The individual who so falls away is
cut off as a branch, and withered ; a particular
Church which tolerates him, reckoning him still
a member, becomes partaker of his sin, and
ceases to be a part of the whole Church of
Christ. The Catholic Church consists of those
who conform to the standard set.

This crude conception contains obvious
elements of truth ; its falsity is conspicuous
when some one fault is made the dividing line.
That happened in the Roman Church of the
third century, when Cornelius restored to communion the *libellatici* of the Decian persecution.
The advocates of a stricter discipline forthwith
renounced him, and procured the election and
consecration of Novatian to be bishop in his
room. The example of Rome was infectious.
Similar schisms sprang up elsewhere, especially
in the East, and those who made this stand for
strictness supported one another by mutual
communion after the fashion of the Catholic

Church. They called themselves the Pure ; they would not be contaminated by communion with any who had even pretended a compromise with idolatry. They seem to have been generally men of high character, and at Nicaea efforts were made in vain to draw them back to Catholic unity. Building on so narrow a base, they were essentially a sect ; they had their own sectarian unity, and they made a sectarian schism. I do not know that they ever claimed expressly to be the whole Catholic Church, but their conduct implied the claim.

That claim was expressly made by the Donatists. Their schism had a similar origin. In A.D. 311, Caecilian was elected Bishop of Carthage. A party in the Church took exception to him on various grounds, chiefly because the bishop who consecrated him was said to be a *traditor*, contaminated by connivance with persecution. Maiorinus, apparently a most worthy person, was elected in his place. What Rome was to the world, and perhaps something more, Carthage was to the African provinces, and within their ambit the characteristics of the Novatian schism were reproduced in a sharper form ; to communicate with Caecilian or with Maiorinus was made the test of Catholicity,

and rival episcopates were set up everywhere.
Donatus, an equally respectable person, suc-
ceeded Maiorinus, and the schism became
inveterate.

At the beginning the Donatists probably had
a good case ; they spoilt it by their subsequent
conduct.   Their assertion that they were maintaining the traditions of St. Cyprian and the
African Church were not unfounded.   But
St. Cyprian's principles allowed the reference
of the dispute to the judgement of a wider
episcopate.   That judgement was given.   A
council of Italian and Gallic bishops, held at
Rome, examined the charges laid against
Caecilian, and found them unproved.   A
larger council, held at Arles in A.D. 314, ruled
that consecration by a *traditor*, even if proved,
would not invalidate his episcopate.   The
Donatists might have appealed to a yet wider
judgement, but they would not.   They stood
by the sufficiency of their own judgement.
They declared that all who sided with Caecilian
became partners of his guilt.   They proclaimed
as a principle the duty of separation from all
such.   " Exite de illa populus meus " became
their watchword.   In accordance with the
African tradition, they rejected even the bap-

tism of their opponents, rebaptizing all who came over to them. It was not enough to treat the adherents of rival bishops in Africa as schismatics, having no part in the Church of Christ ; they extended the same treatment to the flock of any bishop who recognized Caecilian. But all the bishops throughout the world, apart from Africa, were more or less in communion with Caecilian. The Donatists banned them all.

There was a necessary consequence. The Donatists themselves were the whole Catholic Church of Christ. They did not flinch from claiming so much. In the dreary controversy that followed, the dullest and dreariest in the history of the Church, that was the crucial point at issue. There was insufferable wrangling over minor questions, endless discussion of irrelevant texts of Holy Scripture, charge and counter-charge of inconsistency, of violence, of moral depravity ; but there was ultimately one question alone : Were the Donatists the only genuine Christians in the world, or were they schismatic sectaries, wilfully separating themselves from the general body of the faithful ? It must be this or that ; they themselves would have it so. Their opponents scornfully asked whether Christianity was confined to

M

Africa. They replied with wonderful mystical interpretations of Scripture, showing that this was even foreordained, or with practical arguments showing that they and they alone had come out of the City of Destruction. Some men of orthodox belief continued in their company. There was one Ticonius, for whom St. Augustine had a great regard, complaining that he made himself ridiculous by communicating with Donatists while opposing their tenets.[1] There were inconsistencies among them. St. Augustine mentions, on the authority of the same Ticonius, a council held at Carthage, in which they decided that *traditores*— as they called all who held with Caecilian— refusing to be baptized might be admitted to Communion without rebaptism. But to allow this, he said, was to give up their case : the Donatists as a whole considered themselves the whole Church.[2] It was hard, even for them,

[1] *Contra Epist. Parmen.* i. 1 : Ticonius enim omnium sanctarum paginarum uocibus circumtunsus euigilauit, et uidit ecclesiam Dei toto orbe diffusam. *De Doctr. Christ.* iii. 30 : Ticonius quidam qui contra Donatistas inuictissime scripsit, cum fuerit Donatista, et illic inuenitur absurdissimi cordis, ubi eos non omni ex parte relinquere uoluit.

[2] *Ep.* xciii : Si autem uniuersos Donatistas non audimus, se pro ecclesia Christi supponentes, . . . quanto minus, rogo te, Rogatianistas audire debemus ? Below, after

confidently to set Africa against the world ; they tried to establish themselves elsewhere, setting up a bishop at Rome, whose pretensions covered them with ridicule ; it was a vain attempt, for their schism never spread abroad as Novatianism did, and they remained to the end a local African sect.

The principle of separation, their mainstay in argument, produced its natural result. Divisions were rife among them, and every fraction proclaimed the duty of coming out from the rest. For some of them the Catholic Church shrank to a handful of believers in the Numidian hills. Yet they held by a principle of unity no less than by the principle of separation. The good were to be separated from the bad ; that was a cardinal principle ; but divisions among the good were intolerable. There was nothing like that tolerance of sectarianism with which we are now familiar. Those who recognized themselves as the good denounced in unmeasured terms all who broke away from them into dissident sects. When St. Augustine

showing that before the time of St. Cyprian heretics were admitted without rebaptism, he adds : " Qua in re, sicut ingenium tuum noui, facillime perspicis totam causam uestram penitus euersam et extinctam."

rallied them, as he did unmercifully, on their
fissiparous tendency, asking them how they
could blame others who had followed their own
example, they had but one answer ; by the
very act of separation the dissidents showed
that they were not of the number of the good.
He turned this argument upon them with the
remark that the world at large judged them in
exactly the same way.   Mankind will judge
with perfect confidence that those who separate themselves from mankind are no good
men.[1]

Securus iudicat orbis terrarum.   The words
have been frequently quoted, and commonly
misapplied, since Wiseman's famous use of
them in controversy and Newman's more
famous confession of the perturbation which
they caused him.   They must be read with
their context.   It was a practical answer to
a practical question, not a theoretic statement
of the principle of unity.   As a theoretic statement it would be weak.   The Donatists could
reply that, since their own Africa was certainly

---

[1] *Contra Epist. Parmen.* iii. 24 : Quapropter securus
iudicat orbis terrarum bonos non esse qui se dividunt ab
orbe terrarum in quacumque parte terrarum.   See the
argument further developed in my *Catholicity*, App. B.

a part of the world, there was no unanimous judgement of the world against them. Taken in the abstract, therefore, the maxim could mean only that an overwhelming majority of the world is sure to be right. As a mere statement of fact it might stand. An overwhelming majority is at least confident of its own judgement; *securus iudicat*. But St. Augustine neither could nor would build on that. He had a profound respect, perhaps an exaggerated respect, for the general judgement of mankind, but he knew that within living memory Athanasius had been standing firm against a world which groaned to find itself Arian. His appeal to the judgement of the *orbis terrarum* was not the enunciation of an abstract principle; it was a rough application of that principle of unity to which the Donatists themselves bore witness. "You," he said, "a mere party in these African provinces, confidently affirm that it is wrong to break away from you; with how much greater confidence can the world at large condemn you for ostentatiously separating yourselves." He meant that their principle of unity was right, their principle of separation was wrong.

He had a more positive argument. He

continually pressed his antagonists with the parable of the wheat and the tares. To their principle of separation he opposed a principle of comprehension. Under existing conditions the good and the bad were not to be segregated. But what of the discipline of the Church and the power of excommunication ? He made a startling reply. This power must not be used where its exercise will be likely to cause a schism. You must not hope to banish all evil from the Church ; it is useless to condemn a great multitude at once ; faults must be endured with sorrow and sighing, if they are so widespread and so deep-rooted that an attempt to remedy them by severity would rend the Church in twain.[1] He condemns the puritan conception of the Church. For practical purposes he sets the note of unity above the note of holiness.

This tolerance of evil is remarkable. Perhaps you will take it as evidence of a declension from the former austerity of Christian discipline, a result of the compromise with the

[1] *Ibid.* 14 : Neque enim potest esse salubris a multis correptio, nisi cum ille corripitur qui non habet sociam multitudinem. Cum uero idem morbus plurimos occupauerit, nihil aliud bonis restat quam dolor et gemitus.

world which followed the conversion of the Empire. It is the more remarkable in its proper connection, because in dealing with the Donatists St. Augustine departed from his previous judgement to advocate measures of persecution. The victims expressed their abhorrence of such conduct. " May it never be on our conscience," cried one of them, " to compel any man to believe with us." [1] The abjuration was, perhaps, not very sincere, but it accorded with their principle of separation. They had their own kind of intolerance, which differed from Augustine's ; he would compel men to come in, they would thrust men out. His intolerance of schism went with his tolerance of evil. Both alike were directed against the principle of separation.

There is much to be said on the other side. Restrictive theories of unity are not lightly to be condemned. In a measure they are necessary. The Church at large is called to separation from the world, to be a garden enclosed. Where and what is the hedge ? Christianity is not the

[1] *Contra Literas Petiliani*, ii. 83 : "Absit, absit a nostra conscientia ut ad nostram fidem aliquem compellamus." Augustine weakly replies that the imperial laws were not designed to make Donatists good, but to restrain them from doing evil.

religion of the average man, and the Christian
Church is not humanity in the lump. It consists of those who are redeemed in Christ out
of mankind. There must be some definition
of a Christian.

But definition is beset with perils. On the
one hand is the peril of deceptive largeness.
You may extend Christianity by emptying it
of meaning. On the other hand there is
a constant tendency to sectarian narrowness.
It is terribly easy to exaggerate the requirements of orthodoxy, and whenever you add
anything to the definition of a Christian you
must remember that you draw closer the limits
of Christendom. You may ultimately bring
yourself to an absurdity. The Donatists did
that when they added to the definition of
a true Christian the *differentia* of being in
communion with Maiorinus. Far short of
that, you may come within measurable distance
of sectarianism. The great Cappadocians were
right when they refused to restrict the name
of Catholic to the few who stood by Athanasius
in his extremity. They left that sort of madness
to Lucifer of Cagliari.

There is a purely human aspect of catholicity
which must not be overlooked, and the con-

ception of *orbis terrarum* has a larger value than appears in the special argument of Augustine against the Donatists. If the Christian Faith is Catholic in the full sense of universality, because it is intended for all mankind and corresponds to all human needs, no less than because it sets forth the whole counsel of God, it will need for its guardianship the common testimony of all sorts of men. Some will bear special witness to one part of the content, others to another part. The witness of the *orbis terrarum*, of the widest possible combination of humanity, will be needed for the whole. This does not mean that complete unanimity is required, so that nothing can be accounted Catholic which is anywhere impugned. Negligible minorities ought to be neglected. The unity of the Church is not intended to embrace every vagary of thought and practice which claims to be Christian. St. Paul's rough answer to contentious eccentricity, "We have no such custom, neither the Churches of God," is perennially valid. But you must make sure that what you neglect is negligible, and it is idle to pretend that you can do that as easily now as it could be done by the Apostle, or even by St. Augustine. The testimony of the

N

orbis terrarum will not always be as available as it was against the Donatists.

You must not be in a hurry to exclude heretics from the Church. If you are too eager, you may become as sectarian as the heretics themselves. And caution is needed, not only on that ground of expediency which St. Augustine alleged, the fear of schism, but for a less questionable reason also. He pressed against the Donatist principle of separation the warning of the parable, "Lest ye root up the wheat with them." What looks like heresy, what has indeed the heretical temper of self-assertion, may be a valuable witness to some part of the truth. It is a commonplace that heretics of the most definite kind may bring to the support of the common truth a testimony which is the more weighty because of its very separateness and independence. Theologians of the straitest Catholicism—if such a contradictory term may be allowed—will call in aid the witness of ancient separated Churches to show that some detail of belief or practice is no recent innovation; they will even use the consent of modern dissidents to strengthen their argument for a doctrine which they are defending. That is positive testimony. More cautiously they will adduce negative testimony of the same kind. The negations of heretics, old or new, may not count for much, but there are times when they will lend further support to a reasonable doubt whether a doctrine or practice should be regarded as necessary. No heretics can be altogether ignored. They contribute to the sum of Christian witness. Do you object to counting them in as if they were Catholic? I must remind you that we use this word in two senses intimately connected but distinct, neither of which can claim priority in time. That is Catholic which embraces the whole truth of God without partiality; the Church is Catholic also because it embraces potentially the whole of mankind without particularity. There is, therefore, an intensive Catholicity, to which heretics do not attain; there is also an extensive Catholicity in which they have part. The *orbis terrarum* includes them. They must count for what they are worth.

There results from this a limitation of the usefulness of the conception. It served St. Augustine well against the Donatists, but it will not settle every question of schism. There was one that distracted the East during

Augustine's early manhood. Was Meletius
or Paulinus the true Bishop of Antioch ? It
was not unlike the dispute at Carthage, but
there was no united judgement of the Church
beyond the confines of Syria to determine
it. Jerome, vexed with the wrangling which
disturbed the lands where he was seeking
ascetic quietude, found a solution that satisfied
his young soul. The bishop recognized by
the Roman Church should be his bishop.
" I reject Meletius," he wrote to Damasus ;
" I know not Paulinus ; he that gathereth not
with thee scattereth." [1]   But there was no
general consent, leading the one way or the
other, and the schism had to be healed by
the exercise of mutual charity at Antioch.
One is inclined to wonder whether the parties
in Africa might have been less unaccommodating
if the *orbis terrarum* there also had suspended
judgement.

Judgement so conclusive was still less
possible in the case of that schism of the
eleventh century which still continues. The
West separated itself from the East, the East
from the West ; where was the *orbis terrarum*
which could confidently judge either as depart-

[1] *Ep.* xv.

ing from its unity ?   There was the same
difficulty at the time of the Great Schism of
the West ; where was the whole that might
decide between Pope and Antipope and their
contending factions ?   It was not otherwise
with the sharper cleavage of the Reformation.
Disputants appealed to a General Council ;
they were offered the Tridentine ; half of
them refused it, not without reason, as
fundamentally sectarian.   Can you bring to
St. Augustine's test the standing schism of
which the claims of the papacy are the dividing-
line ?   These claims are as exclusive as those of
the Donatists.   The Christians who reject them
are a majority ; but they are a ragged regiment,
and an *orbis terrarum* including none of those
in communion with Rome would be as great
an absurdity as one consisting of them alone.

To the great schisms of history this test
is not applicable.   Yet the conception of the
orbis terrarum, as used by St. Augustine, is not
without abiding value.   It is a witness against
the sectarian principle of unity.   It points to
a large unity, extending ideally to all mankind,
as the true mode of existence for the Church
of Christ.   It is the refutation in principle
of all exclusive claims of a sect.   It is the

condemnation of Puritanism. It indicates
that neither must Christians withdraw into
an enclosure apart, nor must they be zealously
affected to cast out others. Many accidents
may befall the Body of Christ in a wayward
world, but to exalt separation into a principle
is to deny the very substance of the Body.

You should not look for sectarianism in
those sects which you condemn. No doubt
you will find it there, and will condemn it
whole-heartedly. It is more important to look
for it in yourself, and in those with whom you
habitually act. You will find it when you
adopt some facile rule for distinguishing tares
and wheat. You will find it when you employ
some convenient standard, set by the fashion
of the day, for determining what is catholic or
orthodox, enlightened or liberal. Your standard may be a part of the truth of God, but
you can isolate it into a falsehood. Perhaps
nowhere can you stumble more easily into
sectarianism than in the search after unity.
For sectarian unity, the unity of those who
pronounce a *shibboleth* in exactly the same way,
is the easiest thing in the world to achieve. In
despair of achieving a larger unity according to
the will of God—which is one of the hardest

of tasks—you may fall back on that easy course, and lapse into a contentment that is death. Beware of agreements. Agreement to differ is the worst kind ; but agreement on selected articles may be a worse danger. It is a substitute for the unity of the Body of Christ ; and it is a substitute that satisfies.

LECTURE V

INDEPENDENCY AND DENOMINA-TIONALISM

Ye are no more strangers and sojourners, but ye are fellow-citizens with the saints, and of the household of God, being built upon the foundation of the apostles and prophets, Christ Jesus himself being the chief corner-stone ; in whom all building, fitly framed together, groweth into a holy sanctuary in the Lord ; in whom ye also are builded together for a habitation of God in the Spirit.—*Eph.* ii. 19.

I COME to the examination of a conception of the Church which first appeared in England, and which has become characteristic of the English-speaking peoples, until it almost entirely dominates their common religious thought. In some sense, it is acknowledged, there is but one Church of Christ ; but what is seen is in effect a number of independent Churches, more or less acutely differing from one another, sometimes engaged in open rivalry, seldom or never attached to one another by any links of mutual fellowship or co-ordinate action. And this state of things is accepted as normal. The worst features of it are generally condemned ; bitter antagonism is deprecated, the waste of spiritual power is deplored, and the Churches are exhorted to work together in brotherly concord for the good of mankind. But the authors of these expostulations usually take as a matter of course the entirely independent existence of the Churches addressed. Others, having eyes to see how strangely at variance is this state of things with that in which the apostolic foundations of the Church were laid, go further and earnestly advocate some closer union of the Churches, or at least of those which have most in common. But even these start from an independence which is to be surrendered, in whole or in part, for the sake of unity. They build on a conception which may be called by the rather barbarous name of Denominationalism.

What is the origin of this conception ? You may trace it back to a source with which it has no necessary connection, the Reformed doctrine of Equality of Ministers. This was a detail in the general revolt against the developed prelacy of the Middle Ages ; you may, perhaps not unfairly, suppose that it was suggested by

o

the needs of reformers who could not carry the
hierarchy with them ; but another aspect of
it must not be overlooked. It was a revival,
more or less conscious, of the Cyprianic theory
of the equality of bishops. Do not let this
fact be obscured by questions, important in
themselves, about the mode of ordination. In
relation to my immediate subject, the sufficiency of presbyteral ordination, or indeed the
necessity of any ordination, will be a side-
issue. You may say with perfect accuracy that
the Reformed doctrine makes every minister
a bishop. The title may not be used, but
what the title stands for is intended. Where
the system is worked out consistently, you
will find this clearly understood. In Scotland
there is a curiously exact reproduction of the
external order of the Church of Africa. It is
for the most part in miniature. Each Scottish
parish represents an African diocese. Some
of them are at least as large as St. Augustine's
flock at Hippo, but most of them are very
small. Large or small, each of them has one
minster, who corresponds very closely in
function to the bishop of the third century ;
he has under him a college of presbyters or
elders, and usually some deacons ; the ministers

of a district assemble in presbytery, or in a larger synod, and the General Assembly answers to Cyprian's plenary council of the African provinces which dealt with the question of Baptism. The likeness is pressed. The late Dr. Lindsay, in his book on the ministry in the early centuries, ingeniously applied ecclesiastical terms now current in Scotland, spoke of Cyprian calling together his " Kirk-session," and did not forget the "congregational meeting." I think he was justified in this.

So far there is no progress towards Denominationalism. There is but a more minute administrative division of the one Church on the traditional lines. You must now turn to another doctrine which played a great part in the controversies of the Reformation, the doctrine of the Invisible Church, common to Luther, to the Swiss Reformers, and to Calvin. Calvin's strict theory of predestination gave it a special form, but Luther was the inventor of it, and Rudolf Sohm reckons it one of his greatest gifts to the world. According to this doctrine, the true universal Church consists of those souls which are known to the secret counsel of God as redeemed and saved

in Christ out of mankind. They form a holy
society, held together by the operation of the
Spirit. They themselves recognize one another,
if at all, imperfectly ; but their union is none
the less real. The unity of the Church is
absolutely secured.

This invisible Church has no visible counter-
part. There is no outward framework of
human society representing it in its entirety.
But its members, the members of the mystical
Body of Christ, are drawn by their spiritual
affinity into close association. They fall
naturally into groups, determined by external
circumstances. God has so ordained. And
every such group has certain qualities of the
true Church. Where two or three are gathered
together in the Name of Christ, there He has
promised to be in the midst of them. But
where Christ is, there is the Church, his
Body. Every such group may therefore be
called a Church. It is a living image of the
true Church. But since the true members of
the Church are not visibly discerned, others
may creep in unawares, and therefore this
visible Church will be but an imperfect image
of the invisible. Indeed, it may be no Church
at all, but a congregation of Satan masquer-

15094

ading as a Church of Christ. Spiritual things, however, are spiritually discerned, and those who are led by the Spirit will sever themselves from such a society.

The only visible Church of Christ is a particular Church of this kind. It partakes of the qualities of the invisible Church. The invisible Church is Catholic, because of certain qualities which make for universality ; this visible Church has those qualities, and may, therefore, though local and particular, be called Catholic. The invisible Church is holy, a communion of saints, and this visible Church partakes of that holiness. The invisible Church is one, indefectibly united ; this visible Church shares that unity, though imperfectly ; it can be divided, but schism is sin.

What is the constitution of this visible Church? It is a group of individual Christians. It must be capable of assembly, for the gathering together is essential. You must look for something like the City of Aristotle, a small community which can be taken in, so to say, at a glance.[1] It will also resemble the Greek city in respect of autonomy, for this community can do of itself all that can

[1] *Pol.* iv. 4, 14 : εὐσύνοπτος.

be done by any outward image of the invisible Church.

There are two ways in which such a community may be constituted. It may be defined by local circumscription. It will then be the duty of all Christians within a given district to assemble themselves together ; membership in the local visible Church will be obligatory, and the formation of dissident assemblies will be an act of schism. That, as we know, was the general constitution of Christian Churches from the beginning ; it was retained by many of the Reformed, and notably in the Netherlands and in Scotland. The best enunciation of the whole theory will be found in the Belgic Confession.[1]   But there is another way, which seems more consonant with the doctrine of the invisible Church and all its consequences. The visible Church will be a congregation of members freely gathered by their own choice of company. That may seem to go better with the freedom of the spirit. It was the discovery of Robert Browne, and it produced the Independents.

Independency must be studied in its origin. It might have sprung up in any Church polity ;

[1] See Appendix V.

in point of fact, it was a revolt against the English parochial system, as used by Presbyterians. The Nonconformists of the sixteenth and seventeenth centuries, holding the equality of Ministers in the sense of the Reformed Confessions, were determined to get rid of prelacy, but they took into their service the parochial machinery of the Mediaeval Church. It gave them excellent standing ground. In the unwieldy dioceses of the English Church the several parishes were inevitably allowed, in great measure, to manage their own affairs. There was over them an elaborate system of government, rather vexatious than helpful, depending on a remote and inaccessible bishop, who was very far removed from the exercise of the pastoral office. The Nonconformists treated this episcopacy as a mere creation of the law, a kind of magistracy, which had to be endured until a better reformation should remove it. Compromising with it, submitting where submission was inevitable, they tried to organize the parishes under its shadow in a system of classes and presbyteries according to their conception of what the ordering of the Church should be. They treated the

parish as a local particular Church of the
primitive model, aiming at what was actually
effected before their eyes in Scotland. In
doing this they took full advantage of what
measure of independence the parish possessed,
and especially of the position of security
given by law to the incumbent. Robert
Browne saw that this would not do. He
was a hare-brained creature, unstable to the
last degree, and incapable of organizing
anything; but he could grasp a principle, and
he struck a note which reverberated wide and
deep. His *Treatise for Reformation without
tarrying for any*, struck at the Nonconformist
compromise with prelacy as a legal institution.
But he went further. He denounced the use
of the parochial system, with its legal organization and its legal ministry. To accept
this was to allow the legal rights of parish-
ioners; it meant the assumption that every
inhabitant of a parish was presumably a true
member of the true Church of Christ, and
must be treated as such. This was contrary
to the principles of the Gospel, contrary to
the true constitution of the visible Church
as an assembly of the faithful who were
redeemed and called out of mankind. There

must be a new departure. The "gathered Church" which he formed was, perhaps, a mere experiment, a mere protest against existing conditions; but it was formed on a clear and intelligible principle, and it became the model which others followed who had that power of organization which he himself lacked. He brought Independency to the birth.

It was a clear and intelligible principle. I cannot find a better statement of it than that which is given by Neal in his *History of the Puritans*: "Every Church or society of Christians meeting in one place was, according to the Brownists, a body corporate, having full power within itself to admit and exclude members, to choose and ordain officers, and, when the good of the society required it, to depose them, without being accountable to classes, convocations, synods, councils, or any jurisdiction whatsoever." [1]

Is this delirious? To a mind steeped in Catholic tradition it may seem midsummer madness. But if you abstract the lessons of history, you will find something not unlike it in the canonical books of the New Testament. You can apply to the invisible Church of this theory almost

[1] *Hist. of the Puritans*, vol. i, p. 253, ed. 1754.

all references to the Church as one. Then
you have left a number of Churches with
no apparent link but that of brotherly intercourse and a rather indeterminate apostolic
oversight. Assume the apostolate to be a
mere foundation, not a continuous order of
administration, and the disappearance of the
Apostles in the course of nature will leave
these several Churches, gathered on the model
of Independency. Nay, you may think that
you find direct support for this model in
that very Epistle to the Ephesians which
contains St. Paul's most emphatic teaching
about the unity of the Church.

It is in one of the rare passages where
a varied reading has doctrinal significance. In
the English version of the seventeenth century
you read these words : " In whom all the
building fitly framed together groweth unto an
holy temple in the Lord." That goes well with
the argument of the Epistle. But this rendering
supposes a reading of the text which has no
critical support, πᾶσα ἡ οἰκοδομή. The definite
article cannot stand. Without it the most
natural meaning of the phrase will be that which
was adopted by the authors of the Revised
Version, and by your American Committee

working with them—"each several building."
If that is what St. Paul meant, you will have
to revise your reading of the whole epistle.
The building of which he speaks in such
burning words will be the building, not of
the one Church, but of particular Churches;
the union which he acclaims will be nothing
more than brotherly intercourse between
Churches threatened with discord. There is
an escape from this conclusion. The Greek
word will carry another sense. It will stand
for the act of building, and so it is rendered
in the Vulgate, "omnis aedificatio." The
meaning will then be that all work of building
which is done contributes to the completion
of the one sanctuary, the true Church of God.
The general Christian tradition justifies and
requires that rendering; but it cannot be
denied that apart from tradition this text,
like many others, might be read in support
of Independency.[1]

The obviousness of this textual support,
taken apart from Catholic tradition, accounts

[1] Dr. Armitage Robinson deals with this subject very
carefully in his Exposition of the Epistle. I differ by a
hair's breadth from his conclusion. It is curious that
Wiclif should have rendered the Vulgate text " eche
bildynge made."

for the general diffusion of Independency in
England and English-speaking countries. The
Puritan movement ran that way. Presbyterianism took little hold on Englishmen.
As known to them, it was clerical and
academic. It was built on the parochial
system, and the parochial system is in fundamental disagreement with Puritanism.
The Presbyterian Nonconformists denounced
separation; the consistent Puritan sought a
separated Church. Careless of Catholic tradition, strangely indifferent to history, Englishmen yielded themselves for once to the
tyranny of the *a priori*. Independency was
a complete and rounded logical idea, which
they gathered from the text of Scripture.
It became dominant. The Independents
properly so called, and the Baptists, who were
equally committed to the principle of Independency, conquered the inheritance of Non-
conformity, when finally severed from the
historic Church; Presbyterianism languished,
and by separation from the parochial system
lost its proper standpoint. But Independency
was even more vigorous when detached from
the local traditions of English life, from the
lingering influence of the parish church, and

from the pressure of legal uniformity. I dare
not speak in detail of its diffusion here in
America, lest I stumble on unfamiliar ground,
but I think it was by no means confined to
Massachusetts, or even to those who rejected
episcopacy in principle.

Shall we call Independency essentially schismatic? It was bred in schism, a schism recalling
the schismatic temper of the Donatist. The
gathered Church was declared to be the only
true visible Church of Christ ; the principle
of the equality of ministers, logically carried
out to the denial of synodical authority, was
declared to be fundamental. But the conception
of the gathered Church—the Congregational
system, to call it by a name of late growth, as
distinct from the territorial system—is not
inconsistent with unity. The Church is not
tied to a particular mode of organization, and
one method of administrative division may be
as legitimate as another. If I do not misunderstand your methods in this American
Church, what you call a parish is in point
of fact a gathered congregation, and you
bring this under the shield of episcopal
unity. The papacy also can find room in its
close-knit system for exempt jurisdictions, and

for gatherings of the faithful which are not territorial.

You must bear in mind also that Independency is based on a theory of unity. The invisible Church is indefectibly one and united ; each visible Church is to have a corresponding unity of its own. You may reasonably point to the fissiparous tendency shown by almost all societies formed on this model ; but it should be clearly understood that the procedure of separation is normal, and not irregular. Given the hypothesis of Independency, the splitting of a congregation over a personal question or a point of discipline is no more schismatic than the division of a diocese on geographical grounds.

And Independency has a theory of schism. Unreasonable and unnecessary separation is schismatic in process, even if it produces a new Church of full independent rights. Party spirit within a congregation is schismatic ; it is the kind of schism which St. Paul rebuked at Corinth. Above all, denial of the rights of an independent Church is schismatic. Modern Congregationalism has departed from the intolerance of its origins, and acknowledges true Christian Churches of other models. Reciprocal recognition is demanded. It irritates us to be accused of schism by the spiritual descendants of Robert Browne, but we should try to understand their attitude. They complain of our divisive principles, our " unchurching judgements." Let us rebut the charge with understanding, not with mere scorn.

I speak of Independency as if it still existed in full vigour. It does not. It has proved impracticable. On a small scale, in a restricted region, it could work. On the field of the wide world this multiplicity of small Churches becomes absurd. Grouping, at least, is necessary. The result is Denominationalism.

It is a product of Independency, its inevitable outcome, the adjustment of its principle to the obstinate facts of life. The history of the word is instructive. English legislation of the eighteenth century, following the Toleration Act, recognized Dissenters of three denominations, Independents, Baptists, and Presbyterians. So far the words stood only for nomenclature. But these were real groups ; the Presbyterians had a system of combination in working order, and the others found some common action necessary in the administration of certain charities. The three denominations became entities.[1] The older Independency died hard. It was a great force in England within living memory. It still exists in theory, and in trust-deeds, but it has given way in practice to large alliances, tending always to closer union. The highly organized system of Methodism has not indeed been imitated, but it has had great influence on the developments of the last half-century.

Again I speak of England, but your American experience is probably not dissimilar. Your religious conditions, so far as we are acquainted with them, seem to us to be an exaggeration of our own. In all English-speaking countries, and in all lands to which these countries send evangelizing missions, we are confronted with the same state of things. Everywhere are these Denominations.

Distinctions superficially resembling them are not necessarily in conflict with Catholic unity. The history of the great Religious Orders proves it. There is further proof in the Uniat Churches, jealously kept separate in

[1] Johnson quotes from South an earlier approximation to this use of the word. He speaks of philosophy as divided "into many sects and denominations—as Stoicks, Peripateticks, Epicureans, and the like."—*Dict.* s.v. *Denomination.*

many particulars within the unity of the Roman jurisdiction, which have been extended from Europe and the East even to your States. But we must not be deceived by a false analogy. These are but administrative divisions of one Church, the unity of which is constantly in evidence. The Denominations of which I speak are conceived as so many separate Churches. That is their style, and it describes a real state of things. There is a Methodist Church, a Presbyterian Church, a Baptist Church—I neglect subdivisions— each spread throughout the world, and competing, if the word be not too severe, for adherents drawn from the same populations. Methodists can hold an Ecumenical Conference. And this state of things does not offend. It is thought normal. Historically considered, it is an outcome of Independency, and it continues the tradition of Independency; what the Gathered Church was to the sixteenth century, the Denominational Church is to this twentieth century. But the denominational conception has extended far beyond those who are the direct heirs of its originators. The Presbyterians of the seventeenth century denounced Independency, but Presbyterianism

Q

has become in all respects a Denomination. To
the contemporary divines of the English Church
Independency was an abominable schism, and
even more recent upholders of their tradition
have still been in the habit of telling Dissenters
that they are but disorderly and disobedient
members of the one *Ecclesia Anglicana*. But
the denominational idea has now invaded both
our language and our thought. Whenever
you speak of the " Roman Catholic Church "
or of the " Anglican Church " you are doing
homage to its influence, and are probably not
very far from the acceptance of its principle.
You suggest the existence of distinct Churches,
fundamentally independent ; you imply the
abandonment of the foundation of visible
unity.

So we come to a sectional conception of
Christendom. Unity is only of the Spirit, and
it is not sought in anything resembling a bond
of peace. What way is there out of this
anarchy ?

LECTURE VI

INTERCOMMUNION AND FEDERATION

Giving diligence to keep the unity of the spirit in the bond of peace.—*Ephes.* iv. 3.

THERE is some unity of the Spirit. Even in our present state of anarchy the Christian name is not unmeaning. To profess and call yourself a Christian is to acknowledge certain obligations. "Let every one that nameth the name of Christ depart from iniquity." Christendom is a reality. There are Christian standards of thought and action to which we pay at least the homage of hypocrisy. In the recognition of these standards there is a genuine sense of unity. Torn asunder as we are by inveterate schisms, we still retain consciousness of a special relation more intimate than the general brotherhood of mankind. Moreover, the acceptance of these standards is referred to the operation of the divine Spirit. There is something more than moral or intellectual agreement. If it is almost too obvious to say that no man speaking by the Spirit of God will call Jesus accursed, we go to the heart of things when we add that no man can say " Jesus is Lord " but by the Holy Ghost. And if we have so much, at least, of spiritual agreement about the person of our Holy Redeemer, it is by the same divine operation that we are moved to accept in common, however much we differ in our reading of them, the fundamental obligations of the Gospel. There is this unity of the Spirit.

But where is the bond of peace? There is none. Where is it to be sought? There is much seeking. Christian consciences are in a state of revolt against the principle and practice of dissidence. Good ; but revolt is a perilous process. It is often hurried ; it is at the mercy of generous impulses, which sweep away barriers, and with them may obliterate safeguards. Not by every way of seeking peace can you ensue it. I shall examine two ways by which we are urged to go.

The first is the way of intercommunion. It is attractive. It may seem easy. Perhaps it is too easy : not costly enough for a way of penitence.

It is attractive. It has a fine historic basis. From the beginnings of Christianity there was a free interchange of charity between local and particular Churches. It was St. Paul's triumph to secure this as between Jewish and Gentile Christians. Thenceforward the principle was unchallenged ; the faithful of any particular Church ordinarily had an inviolable right to be received as brothers in full communion by any other Church to which they might come.

We must not forget some practical limitations. It was important to be informed about the actual position of strangers professing to be Christians. They had to present their credentials. It is an obscure and much debated question what was *communio peregrina* ; but all the disputing turns on the effect of commendatory letters, or of the lack of them, and even if the authorities cited are concerned exclusively with the clergy, they raise an overwhelming presumption that all the faithful were for some centuries subject to a similar discipline. This discipline has long since passed away. It gave place, when the profession of Christianity became general, to

a presumption that all persons living in a
Christian community were practising Christians.
Other causes have tended to reduce the
meaning of intercommunion for lay people
to the two points of admission to the sacraments and ecclesiastical sepulture ; in all parts
of the Catholic Church it has long been the
custom to refuse these to none but those who
are publicly known to be unbaptized, formally
excommunicated, or guilty of scandalous
offences. Strangers are therefore received
with much facility, except only where strict
inquiries are made about the condition of
persons proposing marriage. Intercommunion
is made easy. The strict fencing of the
Lord's Table is peculiar to some sects of
the narrower kind, and I believe that even
by them it is now very little practised.
Whether in present circumstances it is wise
to retain this facile administration is a question
for the rulers of the Church ; I am speaking
only of what is now customary.

Some exceptional provisions need a moment's
attention. The real and close union of those
who submit to the jurisdiction of the papacy
allows a diversity of rites, and a disciplinary
rule appears to limit the intercommunion of

those who are thus distinguished. I do not know how far the distinction extends, but I understand that ordinarily a Catholic of an Eastern rite is not allowed to communicate at altars of the Latin rite, and conversely. I mention this for the avoidance of over-statement. Normally, with this and similar exceptions, intercommunion is general and unrestrained.

But there is this to be observed. Catholic intercommunion is a corollary of Catholic unity. It is a consequence, not a cause, of union. The unity of the Church does not consist in this, though it is a most con-spicuous element of visible unity. As such, it is impaired, if not entirely destroyed, by what I have called external schism. Where two particular Churches are so dissociated, the mutual interchange of communion ceases. There was possibly never any strict exclusion in such cases, except for the clergy, and there are well-known modifications even of theory. In the history of the troubles of the fourth century intolerable situations occur which are smoothed over by a theory of " mediate communion." If Rome and Antioch were out of communion with each other, while both were in communion with the Churches of Cappodocia, they are held to have been mediately in Catholic communion.

What is there here to help us in our troubles of to-day ? Little or nothing, I fear. We are asked to find a way to unity by intercommunion as between different Denominations. But intercommunion is an expression of existing unity. What unity is there to be expressed and maintained by this bond of peace ? Some unity of the Spirit we must acknowledge, but is it the kind of unity which is naturally expressed by the external bond of a sacrament ?

The existence of Denominations does not necessarily conflict with unity. The Uniat Churches within the unity of the Roman jurisdiction bear me out. They are precisely Denominations, and this character becomes the more pronounced when groups of their members are scattered here in your country. The great Religious Orders, again, are precisely Denominations. Both examples show that the original idea of the episcopal order, the rigid rule of one bishop in one city, the exclusive pastorate of the faithful within a local circumscription, is subject to modification. But Denominationalism means something else. It is not inconceivable that Denominations even of the kind with which we are concerned might be recognized as integral parts of the one Catholic Church, retaining their separate organization and their peculiar qualities. Intercommunion would follow. But is this practicable ? Let us deal with facts as they are.

Let us without false modesty speak of heresy. The Denominations are not separated by a clean schism. That would make reunion difficult enough ; but there is a more serious cleavage. I shall take only two points, for they are sufficient.

These Denominations are in point of fact based on the principle of Independency. I have said what I have to say on that head. It is a denial of the real unity of the visible Church of Christ ; it assumes the existence of real and original Churches formed anew by the congregation of believers. For those who hold by this, intercommunion means an interchange of good offices between separate Churches, not an interchange of charity between members of one and the same Church. It is like the interchange of trade or of courtesies

R

between the peoples of independent sovran states. It is not the same thing as Catholic intercommunion. Do not misunderstand me. If an individual member of such a Denomination desire communion purely as a Christian, as baptized into the Body of Christ, good cause must be shown for refusing him, and to show cause may be difficult ; but if he ask to be received as a Congregationalist, as a Presbyterian, as a Methodist, it is another matter. You must be consistent : if a man calling himself an Anglican desire in that particular quality communion with Christians who are not so described, his right to be received will be, at least, no obvious right. Denominational intercommunion means such obvious right, or it means nothing. Unless it means this, it is no way to the closing up of our divisions.

I turn to my other point : the obstinate question of the sacred ministry. You will find no way of escape in subtle distinctions between validity and regularity. To lay down absolutely what are the essentials of valid ordination is probably beyond the power of any ecclesiastical authority. "The Lord knoweth them that are His;" the secret of acceptability is hidden within the divine knowledge. When a Congregationalist friend said to me, " I reckon myself as good a priest as you, and as good a bishop as the Bishop of London," I had no answer. You cannot show peremptorily that such an one is not a priest of the Most High God. But the pastors of the Church can say, and ought to say, that no man shall be allowed to minister to their flock unless there is ample cause for believing him to be truly admitted to the sacred ministry. They have not to prove a negative against him ; they have to make good the affirmative. And there seems to be only one way of doing this. A man ordained according to the immemorial practice of the Catholic Church needs no further credential ; without this, his title remains at least in doubt.

That is the case with the ministers of certain Denominations. I put the difficulty at the lowest : it is a bar to intercommunion. For intercommunion is nothing if not mutual. It means the acceptance of the ministry of others for our people, as well as the offer of our ministration to others.

I would emphasize this by reference to an attempted solution of the difficulty. The

agreement of Kikuyu, which made so much
noise in the world three years ago, was a one-
sided affair. The Bishops of Mombasa and
Uganda undertook to admit the disciples of
Presbyterian missionaries to their communion,
but they would not allow a Presbyterian mis-
sionary to minister in like manner to their own
people. There was no equality, no mutuality.
Whatever the result might be, it was not intercommunion. There is no intercommunion
here, because there is not that unity of belief
and practice which intercommunion should
express. The case is crucial. Intercommunion
without unity is not a way to reunion. Do
not imagine that sporadic action taken by
individuals will have any effect in this regard.
Intercommunion is not a relation of individuals : it is a relation of communities. It is
best to look facts in the face even if they be
disagreeable. " Better is the sight of the eyes
than the wandering of the desire."

The other remedy for schism that I would
examine is Federation. Speaking to you here,
I need not enlarge on the nature of federal
union ; you live under a federal constitution,
and you understand it. If I were speaking to
men of my own country, much explanation

would be necessary ; for in England the meaning of federation is little understood. Some
of us have learnt from Acton to regard a constitution such as yours with deep respect, as a
most admirable form of political organization,
the surest safeguard against the tyranny of the
absolute State ; but most Englishmen imagine
that your State governments derive their powers
by devolution from the central authority.
Speaking to you, I need but recall the obvious
fact that federation starts from the existence of
a number of sovran States ; federal union is a
junction of originally independent units, which
have agreed to abate their sovranty by delegating
certain powers to a common organ of government.   What place, then, can be found for
the method of federation in the ordering of
the Church of Christ ? The unity of the
Church is original.

So I put it bluntly. But those who advocate
federation have something to go upon. There
is an appearance of federal union in the historic
organization of the Church. The grouping of
dioceses, the provincial system, the patriarchates, lend themselves to the illusion. In passing
from the original equality of bishops, over-
emphasized by St. Cyprian, to these later

developments, you may seem to be watching
a process like the formation of the Achaean
League or the coalescence of your own United
States. There are differences, even on the
surface, but only a practised eye will detect
them. You, who understand that in a federal
union no one State must have authority over
others, will observe the jurisdiction of the
Metropolitan, and its inconsistency with federal-
ism. You, who know what a federal capital
means, will not imagine that in Rome, *principalis
ecclesia*, you see something analogous. But
others may.

An illustration drawn from secular politics
will help us. Federation and Devolution are
contrary processes, and yet they produce very
similar results. Within the British dominions
all subordinate jurisdiction and all local authority
is theoretically devolved from the Crown in
Parliament. This devolution is sometimes not
much more than a legal fiction, but even so
it determines the forms of organization. The
results are various. You have one of them
at your doors. In this continent there exist
side by side the Dominion of Canada, a result
of devolution, and the United States, a result
of federation. Their constitutions are funda-

mentally different, but superficially similar ; so similar that men who are not familiar with their working fail to see the difference : in England it is customary to speak of Canada as an example of federation.

Devolution is the method of the Church. All authority was concentrated in the upper room of Pentecost. Thence it has been devolved. The origin of diocesan episcopacy is obscure, but only two hypotheses deserve attention. Either it is a modification of the presbyterate appointed by devolution from the Apostles, or it is a continuation of the apostolate as a distinct order. The absolute equality of bishops taught by St. Cyprian might have been a basis of federal union, if he had not taught along with it the equally absolute unity of the episcopate as a whole, each member of it holding *in solidum* an undivided partnership. You cannot federate those who are already essentially one ; nor could any bishop, according to his theory, make that abatement of his own powers in favour of a common authority which is the formative procedure of federation. And further, as we have seen, St. Cyprian's theory does not answer exactly to the facts even of his own time. The authority of councils cuts across it. A council, a group of bishops more or less adequately representing the united episcopate, can depose a bishop ; and so there is already subordination, not created by a sur-render of powers, but inherent in the scheme of things. On the authority of councils super-vened that of the Metropolitan. Its appearance was probably due to considerations of mere convenience, and it followed the lines of imperial organization ; its origin is obscure, but the conciliar decrees of the fourth century make its character plain. You are not to think of the Metropolitan as the chosen head of a province ; it is rather a case of the province being made subordinate to the Metropolitan ; his authority was devolved from that of the united episcopate. The like origin of the Patriarchate is much clearer. And what of the universal authority of the Papacy ? Suppose it to exist, and there are only two possible accounts of it to be given. Either the doctrine of the Vatican Council is true, and then all powers in the Church are devolved from the Pope, or the teaching of thoroughgoing Gallicans must be accepted, and then the Pope is subordinate to a General Council, and his authority is derived by devo-lution from the universal episcopate. Whatever he may be, he is not a federal chief like the King of Prussia in Germany.

I am tempted to say a word about your American episcopate. Forgive me if my imperfect information leads me into mistakes. The ordering of the Church has always been coloured by that of civil society. This influence was conspicuous in the Roman Empire ; less conspicuous, but considerable, in the age of feudalism. It would be strange if you entirely escaped it. You are full of the democratic spirit, and you live under a federal constitution. I think there is some effect visible in your ecclesiastical organization. But the more closely I look into it the less of this I see. The bishops in your General Convention seem to form a Council of the Cyprianic or African model, with the senior, *primae sedis*, presiding. They retain their equality unimpaired, and they bow to no central authority, no federal chief. You may imitate some of the forms of federation, but you have nothing of the essential form.

The apparent precedents for federation, therefore, disappear on a close view. But why not make a precedent ? Why not bring out from the storehouse of the Church things new as

well as things old ? There can be no objection,
if we are quite sure that these new things are
in the storehouse. Are there in the Church of
Christ materials out of which a federal union
can be constituted ? We have to face the fact
of division. Various Denominations exist,
and are sharply divided from each other.
Allowing that some unity of the Church there
is, can we say that these Denominations are
now so completely separated that federation
is the natural way of bringing them together ?
Is this the bond of peace by which we should
establish and maintain the unity of the Spirit ?
The history of your States may once more
illustrate the question. The British Colonies
on these shores had a unity of origin, and
some measure of political unity as depending
on the British Crown ; circumstances drew them
more or less apart from each other ; when each
and all declared their independence they became
separate sovran States, and their only practicable
basis of union was found to be federation. That
process was unknown to the constitution under
which they had been living ; there was no precedent for it ; new conditions required new
methods. Does the analogy hold good in the
present state of Christendom ?

It is an attractive proposition. There seems to be a way out of an intolerable position. For the purpose of examining it I will put aside those questions of doctrine and of the sacred ministry which we have found embarrassing, and will assume that all the Denominations to be federated are agreed in matters of faith and practice. I then observe that true federation is intended, not any colourable imitation. Evidence of this stands out in the resolutions adopted by a Conference at Mansfield College, Oxford, last summer.[1] They speak of a Federal Council having only such limited powers as may be committed to it by the federated bodies. That will show you at once how true the Conference was to the federal idea. This was only an incident, you may say, in a great movement towards federation. True ; but it was an important incident, and I think we may take it to be characteristic of the whole movement. I further observe that federation, thus intended, is properly based on the principle of Independency. I have tried to show that most of the Denominations with which we have to do are logically and historically products of that principle. True to them-

[1] See Appendix VII.

selves, they stand as Independent Churches, and as such they are proper material for federation. Independence is a necessary antecedent to federal union.

There is this also to be considered. It is a fundamental postulate of Independency that the original unity of the Church, the unity of which we speak in the Creed, is invisible. It is unity purely of the Spirit. The visible Church is nothing else but a number of independent congregations. Federal union is therefore the only kind of visible unity that is practicable, the only available bond of peace. But now the ground is shifting under our feet. Federation is no longer a device for treating present disorders ; it is put forward as the fundamental constitution of the Catholic Church.

It is hard to say in which aspect we are called upon to consider it, nor is it necessary for my purpose to decide between them. There is a fatal bar to the acceptance of Federation, either as a principle or as a policy. But we must make our ground sure. Objections may be raised which are not fatal. If we show that precedents supposed to be drawn from the past history of the Church are misleading, and that no true federal system has ever existed, this may suffice to refute the assertion —should it be made—that such a constitution is necessary ; but we have not proved its impossibility under new conditions. Devolution and Federation are contrary movements, but a combination of them is not inconceivable. Again, the intermingling of Denominations, with which we are now familiar, is not an absolute bar to a federal union. We think of federation chiefly in terms of geographical units, but other terms are equally possible. The Church has been organized in the past mainly on geographical lines, with a jealous maintenance of complete unity within a circumscription ; but the rule of one bishop in one city, however useful in safeguarding unity, is not essential. You have but to remember the obscure sharing of functions between St. Peter and St. Paul, and you see that variations of it were possible from the first. Those Uniat rites of which I have spoken supply modern instances ; there are, I think, five Patriarchs of Antioch recognized equally at Rome. The circumstances of your country, whither all the Churches and all the schisms of Europe have been transplanted, make havoc of the rule.

A stiff adherence to episcopal theory would involve minute investigation as to the priority of this or that hierarchy in every corner of the continent, with charges and counter-charges of intrusion even more absurd. It is a scene of confusion, and your calling of God is to reduce it to order ; but you may have to find a new form of unity, based on something other than territorial jurisdiction. This new thing is not impossible. If federation be the right procedure, it will not be hindered by the fact that the units to be federated are locally intermingled. Let us clear our minds, therefore, of these removable difficulties.

When they are removed there remains a bar. I put it to you as an absolute bar. It is the conception of Independency. This conception is essential to the method of Federation ; the units must be independent before they can be conjoined in a federal union. And I put it to you that this conception cannot be accepted. It involves a denial of the visible unity of the Church. The policy of Federation, therefore, involves the same denial. There is no mending of matters that way. You cannot restore the integrity of a seamless robe by turning it into a garment of patchwork. You cannot close

up the schisms of the Church by denying its
fundamental and essential unity.

These two very attractive proposals will not
stand the fire of criticism. Neither Intercommunion nor Federation will solve our
difficulty. If you allow the value of my
criticism, things may seem to be getting desperate. Old and venerable theories of unity
are found to be inconsistent with facts. New
proposals for the attainment of union are
found to be inconsistent with fundamental
theory. We are left with a belief in the visible
unity of the Church and the spectacle of a dis-
united Christendom. I hope you will not
expect me to propound a scheme of my own
for the rebuilding of Jerusalem. " Non ea
uis animo ; " I have not sufficient audacity.
But a little more work of theory—of theory
about facts—remains to be done. Investigation of things as they are may disclose a door
of hope, not indeed standing open, but patient
of being forced—for the Kingdom of Heaven
suffereth violence—or of being unlocked with
understanding.

LECTURE VII

BROTHERHOOD

Sirs, ye are brethren.—*Acts* vii. 26.

I HAVE said that any attempt at federal union involves a denial of the visible unity of the Church. But where is that unity? Is it anything more than playing with words to speak of it as existing? And if it does not exist, what harm is there in a formal denial of it. Why not face facts? Why not acknowledge that the Church is broken to pieces? Beat your breast and acknowledge that in breaking it you have broken the commandments of God; say that this sin of schism, like all sin, is done against God's will; but do not let us pretend that we have not done it. We have done this thing; let us undo it. We have broken the one Church of God into fragments: let us bring them together as best we may.

So you may challenge me, and I must reply. I have to show that the visible unity of the

Church exists, and is the principle of Christian union.

The Church of Christ is a human society. It is not a dream, an ideal to which we may distantly approach ; it is a concrete reality. It began historically as the Remnant of Israel, destined to carry on the tradition of the nation. We see it developing in history, a highly-organized community. And it is One. It has, therefore, a corporate unity, and not a spiritual unity alone.

But this society is not merely human. I mean that it is not a creation of human thought and action. A distinction is necessary. We are familiar with two kinds of human association ; you may call them natural and voluntary. Do not misunderstand me ; what a man does by voluntary action he does in the strength of his nature, subject to the will of God the Creator, and therefore with a power not altogether his own. It is this power which makes every human association, even the most casual and transient, something more than a gathering of individuals. But, in spite of this, one does recognize the voluntary character, let us say, of a club, a society into which a man enters of his own will and the will of his fellows, and

T

from which he can usually withdraw himself at his own pleasure. Set over against this the family, the primary and typical form of natural association. A man is born into it, and he cannot sever the link which binds him to it. The distinction of natural and voluntary is not sharp and absolute, for human life is not divided into compartments by impermeable walls ; as nature enters into the formation of a voluntary association, so the will enters into the formation of one that is natural ; the family begins with marriage, and marriage with a voluntary contract of man and woman. Yet, in the result, the distinction is good, and the two types are easily recognized. The Church is a natural association.

You may prefer to call it supernatural, but that will not affect my argument. Supernature is but a kind of nature, equally with all nature the work of God. The point is that you are brought into a society of this kind not by your own choice, not by your own act, but by an act of God. Such a society is the Church. So it is declared in the record from the beginning : " They that received the word were baptized, and there were added in that day about three thousand souls. . . . And the Lord added to

them day by day those that were being saved."
The Church began as the Remnant, the
true Israel. This nation, the ideal family of
Abraham, had its proper unity, marked by
natural birth and by the covenant of circumcision. Into this stock, says St. Paul—who
evidently knew little of arboriculture, and
inverted the ordinary process—are engrafted
the wild olive-branches of the Gentiles. The
result is an organic whole, a living unity,
a work of God. As such it is in the visible
order of nature. A family, a nation, is in this
sense visible. It is visibly one. The nation
of Israel was visibly one, the more so when
the unfaithful fell away and the Remnant
alone was left. There is nothing to indicate
any variation of this character when the
Remnant expands into the Catholic Church
of Christ. It is an organic unit in the visible
order of nature.

The unity of the Church appears in various
metaphors. It is a building compact of living
stones ; it is the assemblage of the branches of
a vine, it is the Body of Christ. But without
metaphor it is the People of God. And since
the nation is both historically and ideally a
development of the family, so the Church

is spoken of in terms of family. Its members
are brothers. It seems to have been one of
the earliest names by which they were known—
" the Brethren."

What is implied in Brotherhood ? It is an
indestructible relation. Brothers do not cease
to be brothers when they are divided by a
family quarrel. Nor does the family cease to
be one because it is divided. An errant
brother who breaks away from family ties
does not cease to be a brother. When the
Prodigal was riotously wasting his substance
in a far country, the home-keeping elder
brother no doubt regarded him as an outcast ;
so too he regarded himself in his days of
shame ; but the father's heart yearned over
him, and acknowledged him as son with indefeasible right : " This thy brother was lost,
and is found."

Consider how the doctrine of baptism
illustrates this aspect of the Church. It is
generically a sacrament of initiation, common to
many religions. It is a washing away of sin,
symbolic and real. It is specifically a sacrament
of union with the death of Christ. But more
conspicuously it is a sacrament of regeneration, a new birth. This notion of the new

birth, so prominent in the Johannine doctrine, is fundamental : " Except a man be born anew, he cannot see the Kingdom of God." It is not peculiarly Johannine. The coming of the Kingdom is in the eschatological discourses a *palingenesia*.[1] St. Paul can speak of himself as begetting those whom he has won to the faith ;[2] and yet, on the other hand, the life into which they are born is an original creation of God : " If any man be in Christ, he is a new creature." The true life of the Christian, the life which he now lives in the flesh, springs from this origin. So baptism, the initiation into that life, is " the washing of regeneration." You turn to the Epistle of St. Peter, and find the love of the brethren, the characteristic Christian charity, based on this : " Love one another from the heart fervently, having been begotten again, not of corruptible seed, but of incorruptible."[3] There is the assertion of indefeasible brotherhood.

The brotherhood of the Old Testament rested on the twofold basis of natural birth from the seed of Abraham and the covenant

---

[1] Matt. xix. 28.   [2] 1 Cor. iv. 15 ; Philem. 10.
[3] 2 Cor. v. 17 ; Tit. iii. 5 ; 1 Pet. i. 22.

of circumcision. The one determined the
form of the idea, but was not essential in
practice, for there were proselytes ; the other
was the visible sealing of the birthright,
inherited or granted, and was deemed essential.
In the New Testament there is a similar fact
and signature of the fact. But here the
supernatural birth is essential ; the sacramental
signature is obligatory, but not in the same
sense necessary. Apart from what the ancients
called the baptism of blood in martyrdom, you
must take account of the pregnant declaration
of Innocent III in the case of a priest who
was discovered after his death to have been
unbaptized : " Inasmuch as he lived in the
faith of Holy Church and in the confession
of the Name of Christ, we unhesitatingly
declare that he is freed from sin, and has
attained to the joy of the heavenly father-
land." [1]   There is a baptism of desire. Allow
for this, and you have the true foundation of
Christian unity. It stands in the new birth,

[1] 3 *Decr. tit.* 43 *c.* 2 : Inquisitioni tuae taliter respon-
demus : presbyterum quem sine unda baptismatis extremum
diem clausisse significasti, quia in sanctae matris ecclesiae
fide et Christi nominis confessione perseuerauerit, ab
originali peccato solutum et caelestis patriae gaudium esse
adeptum asserimus incunctanter.

by which we are born as brothers in the family of God. Call it, with St. Peter, a holy nation; call it, with St. Paul, *ecclesia*, in the twofold sense of the people and of the assembly; call it, in modern fashion, a society; the fact remains that the Church is primarily a family, a brotherhood. And since the new birth is normally effected, exceptions apart, by means of a sacrament, a visible sign, it follows that this brotherhood, this family, this people, this nation, is visibly one. It consists of those who are regenerate and born anew of water and of the Holy Ghost.

This one family is torn by schism. Frequent enough, sadly frequent, is discord in a family. Is the family therefore severed into two families, or can one part claim to be the whole? Brothers may quarrel atrociously; do they therefore cease to be brothers, or can one cast out another from the brotherhood? Let us get this clear. Schism is trouble within the Church. The word first appears in this connection where St. Paul is dealing with disturbances at Corinth. " I beseech you, brethren," he says, " that there be no schisms among you." He has heard that when they are actually come together for their general

meeting there are schisms among them. He
sadly notes the inevitableness of this. Men
being what they are, " even heresies there
must be among you "—sects and factions
worse than simple quarrels ; and some good
will come of it, he says, for men will be tried
and found stable. Diversities of gifts are
provided expressly " that there may be no
schism in the body, but that the members
may have the same care one for the other." [1]
That original teaching must govern what comes
afterwards. Schism is within the Church.

Yet there is another aspect of schism, or
another consequence. Diotrephes, who loved
to have the pre-eminence and pretended to
cast men out of the Church, may be the first
of those militant schismatics who from the age
of the Donatists to our own time have imitated
his methods ; but he probably did no more
than pervert or exaggerate a procedure already
established. The writer who complains of his
violence writes also of certain persons who
" went out from us." He implies a voluntary
withdrawal, a desertion of the Church, and it
is complementary to that casting out which he

---

[1] 1 Cor. i. 10 ; xi. 18, 19 ; xii. 25. The words
ἐν ὑμῖν and ἐν τῷ σώματι are conclusive.

attributes to Diotrephes. But observe that he
draws an inference : " They went out from us,
but they were not of us (for if they had been
of us they would have continued with us), but
they went out to show that not all are of us."
The phrasing is obscure, but the general
meaning is clear. There were some within the
brotherhood who were not truly of the brotherhood. They were of those who " crept in
privily," a phrase recalling St. Paul's complaint
of " false brethren privily brought in." Elsewhere we read of " false teachers who shall
privily bring in sects of perdition." There is
an implication of false pretence from the first.[1]

Yet it cannot be doubted that these men
were of the number of the baptized. They
were in the same case with Simon Magus. Is
it suggested that in their case the sacrament,
for lack of some due intention, was inoperative ?
That interpretation would fit in with a far
distant development of theology, and we may
find here consciousness of a truth that was
afterwards formulated. But we cannot in this
way dispose of the words in the Epistle to

[1] 3 S. John 9–10 ; 1 S. John ii. 19 ; S. Jude 4 ; Gal.
ii. 4 ; 2 S. Pet. ii. 1. The word "privily" fits equally
well παρεισδύειν and παρεισάγειν.

the Hebrews about "those who were once enlightened and tasted of the heavenly gift, and were made partakers of the Holy Ghost . . . and then fell away." That indicates a real cleavage separating from the brotherhood those who were really brothers.

Here is something different from the schism within the body of which St. Paul speaks. We are on the track which leads to the definite doctrine of St. Cyprian, that heretics and schismatics are so utterly separated from the Church as to be incapable of conveying the gifts of grace : baptism administered by them is naught. In this respect the Donatists were his logical followers. Attention to a hint that the methods of Diotrephes are not to be imitated might have prevented these excesses ; but it was apostolic teaching, interpreted in a one-sided fashion, which gave them birth. Moreover, we have not to reckon only with the specific error of St. Cyprian, condemned by the common sense of the Church, or with the passions of Donatism. Nothing is more usual in the whole range of Christian literature than to speak of schism as separation from the Church. I would, however, put in a word of caution, for in this sense are quoted some texts which do not necessarily bear it. To say that a man is separated *ab unitate ecclesiae*, or *a communione fidelium*, is not the same thing as to say that he is definitely excluded from the Church. If there be an authority which is the appointed link of unity, then to repudiate that authority is to depart from unity, but it is not necessarily a departure from the society which ought to be united under that authority. The prodigal of the parable separated himself wilfully from his father, and demanded a separate share of the goods of the family, and yet he did not cease to be a member of the family. But after abstracting all such modified phrases we may still find abundant instances of a definite assertion that schismatics are definitely separated from the Church.

The result is a puzzle. Those who make the assertion do not follow St. Cyprian. His doctrine was logically coherent ; theirs is not. They allow that these schismatics, hypothetically excluded from the Church, can administer the sacraments of the Church, can give their suffrages, as I have already pointed out, in ecclesiastical elections, and can be subject to the internal discipline of the Church.[1] Here is

[1] *Supra*, pp. 60–62.

the puzzle. How can the same person, at the same time, be excluded from the Church and acting within the Church ? We are not to ask for a perfectly coherent theory of the Church. To ask for that is to suppose a mystery of God reduced within the exact compass of human thought. But an incoherence of this kind is hardly tolerable.

I think it can be reduced. I go back to that First Epistle of St. John, where separation is so sharply accentuated. Who are the separated ? " As ye have heard that antichrist cometh, even now have there arisen many antichrists." These are they who " went out from us, but were not of us." Antichrist is identified : " This is the antichrist, he that denieth the Father and the Son;" and again, "Every spirit which confesseth not Jesus is not of God : and this is the spirit of the antichrist." I turn to the illustrative texts which I have cited, and find the men who have crept in privily identified as those who "deny our only Master and Lord, Jesus Christ." The sects of perdition are the school of those who "deny even the Master that bought them." Here is something very different from those quarrels among believers, that dividing of Christ which St. Paul called

schism. In a kindred passage of the Second
Epistle to the Thessalonians you will find
the governing word to describe this defection,
this denial of the Master. It is apostasy.[1]
It might have been well if Christian writers
had stuck to St. Paul's use of words, calling
by the name of schism only that kind of
division which is within the Church, and
calling separation from the Church by the
name of apostasy. But it is useless to quarrel
with the history of language, and here there
is no need. For apostasy is both heresy
and schism ; there it begins ; but it is not
every heresy or schism that cuts men off from
the Church, it is that only which proceeds to
apostasy, to the denial of the Name of
Christ.

We may now see our way out of a theological difficulty. We shall no longer be
puzzled to understand how some schismatics
can be acting within the Church while others
are said to be excluded from the Church.
There is a real difference. We shall be rescued
from the impossible absurdity of saying that
there are some Christians who are not members
of the Christian Church. What is a Christian

[1] 2 Thess. ii. 3 : ἐὰν μὴ ἔλθῃ ἡ ἀποστασία πρῶτον.

but one who is in Christ, a member of Christ's
Body ? To schismatics who are apostate we
must refuse the name of Christian ; in act,
if not in word, they themselves refuse it.
Schismatics who confess Christ must, on the
other hand, be included within the Church.
We must assume their baptism, unless there
be evidence to the contrary, and we shall
remember that in abnormal cases they may be
within the Church even if unbaptized.

You may stumble here again upon the
question of Catholicity. Is not the Church
Catholic, and are schismatics Catholic ? I shall
have to remind you once more that the word
has two senses. Heretics and wilful schismatics
are certainly not Catholic in the intensive sense,
but they are members of the Church of Christ
which is Catholic by extension. And this may
lead us to the humbling thought that we are
all more or less schismatic. If not wilfully,
then by misfortune or by the fault of others,
we are divided from one another in the Body
of Christ. Yea, Christ is divided.

Shall I dare to propose a remedy ? A formal
remedy, no ; it is not difficult to criticize
proposals that are put forward, and the very
ease of it dissuades me from adding to their

number ; but I do seem to be finding a way by which we may go in search of what is needed.

When the Christian Church, existing in the concentrated community of Jerusalem, was threatened with its first schism, the appointment of the Seven—deacons we may not unreasonably call them by anticipation—was intended to provide a remedy. In point of fact it did something more ; it produced the first Christian apology. The defence of Stephen the protomartyr is noteworthy for many reasons ; not least because among the witnesses against him was the young man Saul. There is good reason for supposing the report contained in the Acts of the Apostles to be an accurate record of what was said. There are certain lapses of memory about details of the familiar writings of the Old Testament, which would be natural in a speech extemporaneous and made under stress of emotion, but which would hardly be overlooked in a literary composition. It is not far-fetched to suppose that the author of the Acts had the record from St. Paul himself. But that is by the way. What I would insist upon is the fact that in the Apology of St. Stephen you have adumbrated that doctrine of the Faithful Remnant which St. Paul afterwards developed in his doctrine of the Church. You can see what the speaker was coming to when he was suddenly interrupted. I fasten, however, on one particular phrase : " Sirs, ye are brethren ! " Observe what the speaker is doing. He is making a breathless survey of the sacred history, seizing the salient points ; yet he stops to recall an apparently trivial incident, the attempt of Moses to reconcile two quarrelling Israelites in Egypt. He does not merely recall it ; he lingers over its details. Why ? Because of its significance. Here was one of the periodic crises in the story of Israel, one of those days of judgement and of sifting with which the story abounds. The traditional Moses of the Exodus is anticipated : " He supposed that his brethren understood how that God by his hand was giving them deliverance." Hence, " Sirs, ye are brethren ! " If all were to be saved, they must realize their brotherhood. If they would not, there would still be salvation—for the holy seed must be preserved—but only for a remnant.

To-day the expostulation of Moses rings in our ears, " Sirs, ye are brethren ! " Few things are more characteristic of our time than the decay of old and bitter controversies. What does it mean? Is it nothing but a loss of interest in things disputed? Is our mutual tolerance the fruit of sheer indifference? There is much of that; but there are signs of something better. Controversies have been thrashed and thrashed again in polemic until there is nothing more to be said, but it is not mere lassitude that supervenes. That might be a worse disaster than mutual persecution. If Christian men ought to live in mutual charity —and the proposition is incontestable—there can hardly be anything worse than to settle down content with inveterate divisions. Agreement to differ is a mockery of unanimity. The Christian ideal is a multitude of one heart and one soul. To forget quarrels will be small gain if the concord that quarrels have broken be left in a deeper oblivion. But we are not to be a prey to dull forgetfulness. There is movement. There is the sound of a going in the tops of the trees. We have come to mutual tolerance, mutual respect. That is so far good, but it is not the same thing as love of the brethren, and it may be a dangerous substitute. More is stirring.

There is a cry not merely for peace, which may
be a sluggish state, but for unity of effort, for
united testimony.   Christian men are learning
that internecine quarrels which leave them
exhausted are worse than internecine ; the
Name of God is blasphemed among the Gentiles through them ; the Church's witness to
the world becomes ineffective, and those who
should be aggressive cannot even hold their
own.   Union is demanded.   The need is felt,
and it is moving men to action.

Here is the hope of our day.   Effort succeeds to aspiration.   Efforts may be ill-con-
ceived, ill-directed ; but they are better than
apathy.   The nature of Christian unity may
be misunderstood, but union is sought.   To
believe in the operation of the life-giving Spirit
within the Body of Christ is to be assured that
all such movement springs from that divine
source.   Therefore men act, however unconsciously, on the true principle of unity.   They
are stirred to a sense of brotherhood.   But,
indeed, is this unconscious ?   Of what are we
more conscious in this new temper of ours
than of brotherhood ?   Mutual toleration is
good ; it is preparatory ; we are going beyond
it ; forbearing one another in love makes way

for diligence upholding the unity of the Spirit in the only bond of peace.

It is this that gives value even to the most ill-directed endeavours after union. I will refer once more to that Conference at Mansfield College of which I have already spoken. Those men who came together with a scheme of federation note in their official record, with noble inconsistency, their desire for " the fuller and closer investigation of their essential unity in faith and effort." Essential unity? They wish to investigate it? Then it is a fact. Then why federation? They have already something better, something more vital. That vital reality underlies the ill-considered overture of Kikuyu. It underlies the dangerous indifference which is replacing the bitterness of sectarian religion. It underlies individual and irregular attempts at intercommunion. All these things have this much of good in them, that they bear witness to the reality of Christian brotherhood.

This general Christianity is not a common foundation upon which different Churches are built. It is not discovered by elimination of differences. A negative undenominationalism of that kind is worthless. What we see at

work is a positive principle, put into operation
more or less incompletely in all sections of
Christendom, and the same in all. It is a
religious principle. The Bishop of Zanzibar,
who is supposed to be stiff in opinions, has
lately said that we should put the unity of the
Church on a religious, not on a theological
basis. That is good advice. It is not easily
followed, for we mix more readily in the
study of theology than in the practice of
religion. Abstract discussion brings together
men whom religious observances hold apart ;
we read one another's books, and hear one
another's lectures, when we are not able to join
in common worship. We are therefore inclined
to look for unity in a theological scheme.
That, I think, is the weakness of the famous
Quadrilateral agreement borrowed by a Lambeth Conference with imperfect understanding
from a declaration made by your American
episcopate.[1] It is too schematic. Real unity
must be found first ; theological and canonical
schemes of union will follow.

The real unity of the Church is sacramental.
I do not mean that it stands in this or that
sacrament. The Church itself is the *sacra-*

[1] See Appendix VI.

mentum unitatis. It is a visible human society informed by divine grace. For this reason jurisdiction is a poor basis of unity, not being sacramental. Government is a *charisma*, a gift of grace, but not an endowment of sanctifying grace. Jurisdiction is vested in the hierarchy, but not on the same footing as the ministry of the Word and the Sacraments. It belongs rather to the good ordering than to the essence of the Church. Of the hierarchy itself you may say that it is rather an instrument of union than the foundation of unity. It is not on that account the less necessary, but the valuation is different. Most schemes of union fly after effects, neglecting causes. The Conferences on Faith and Order, which your Church has instituted, are conceived, I think, on sounder lines. Your nation feels the effect of dis-union more than most, and it is for you to take the lead in promoting those mutual understandings that must precede all efforts after union. From you goes out to the Christian world the reminder, " Sirs, ye are brethren ! "

Brethren. Brothers do not cease to be brothers when they are divided by a family quarrel. Nor does the family cease to be one

because it is divided.   Nor can you rebuild it
on federal principles.   Not federation, but
whole-hearted reconciliation is needed.   The
Christian Church is one family, and Christians
are brothers.   It is a fact, not an aspiration.
All Christians are brothers.   Orthodox and
heretic, Catholic and schismatic, all are brothers.[1]
It is because they are brothers that heresy
and schism are sins.   We are, in point of
fact, one divided family, and the first step
towards reconciliation is the acknowledgement
of brotherhood.   That means repentance.   We
need not look curiously into the origins of
schism ; that is the way to self-exculpation.
We are not called to the easy and pleasant but
unprofitable task of lamenting the sins of our
fathers, and building the tombs of the prophets
whom they slew.   We are called to repent of
our own sins ; not of one another's sins, but of
our own ; the sins by which we have perpetuated discord.   And repentance means
renunciation.   We are not to cast away things
tried and proved, in a vain hope of mutual
accommodation ; but there are sacrifices to be
made before those things are approached.   A
sacrifice should be the giving of something that

[1] See Appendix II, § 6.

we value, something of cost.   And it must be offered, not in hope of gain—for then it is no sacrifice—but as an act of love.   We must listen to the cry, albeit raised by discordant voices, " Sirs, ye are brethren ! "

APPENDIX I

ST. IGNATIUS ON THE EPISCOPATE

I HAVE collected here for convenient reference the most important passages of the Epistles of St. Ignatius dealing with the office and function of a bishop. The text is Funk's.

Ephes. ii–v.

Ὀναίμην ὑμῶν διὰ παντός, ἐάνπερ ἄξιος ὦ. πρέπον οὖν ἐστὶν κατὰ πάντα τρόπον δοξάζειν Ἰησοῦν Χριστὸν τὸν δοξάσαντα ὑμᾶς, ἵνα ἐν μιᾷ ὑποταγῇ κατηρτισμένοι, ὑποτασσόμενοι τῷ ἐπισκόπῳ καὶ τῷ πρεσβυτερίῳ, κατὰ πάντα ἦτε ἡγιασμένοι.

Οὐ διατάσσομαι ὑμῖν ὡς ὤν τις. εἰ γὰρ καὶ δέδεμαι ἐν τῷ ὀνόματι, οὔπω ἀπήρτισμαι ἐν Ἰησοῦ Χριστῷ. νῦν γὰρ ἀρχὴν ἔχω τοῦ μαθητεύεσθαι, καὶ προσλαλῶ ὑμῖν ὡς συνδιδασκαλίταις μου. ἐμὲ γὰρ ἔδει ὑφ' ὑμῶν ὑπαλειφθῆναι πίστει, νουθεσίᾳ, ὑπομονῇ, μακροθυμίᾳ. ἀλλ' ἐπεὶ ἡ ἀγάπη οὐκ ἐᾷ με σιωπᾶν περὶ ὑμῶν, διὰ τοῦτο προέλαβον παρακαλεῖν ὑμᾶς, ὅπως συντρέχητε τῇ γνώμῃ τοῦ θεοῦ. καὶ γὰρ Ἰησοῦς Χριστός, τὸ ἀδιάκριτον ἡμῶν ζῆν, τοῦ πατρὸς ἡ γνώμη, ὡς καὶ οἱ ἐπίσκοποι, οἱ κατὰ τὰ πέρατα ὁρισθέντες, ἐν Ἰησοῦ Χριστοῦ γνώμῃ εἰσίν.

Ὅθεν πρέπει ὑμῖν συντρέχειν τῇ τοῦ ἐπισκόπου γνώμῃ, ὅπερ καὶ ποιεῖτε. τὸ γὰρ ἀξιονόμαστον ὑμῶν πρεσβυτέριον, τοῦ θεοῦ ἄξιον, οὕτως συνήρμοσται τῷ ἐπισκόπῳ, ὡς χορδαὶ κιθάρᾳ. διὰ τοῦτο ἐν τῇ ὁμονοίᾳ ὑμῶν καὶ συμφώνῳ ἀγάπῃ Ἰησοῦς Χριστὸς ᾄδεται. καὶ οἱ κατ' ἄνδρα δὲ χορὸς γίνεσθε,

ἵνα σύμφωνοι ὄντες ἐν ὁμονοίᾳ, χρῶμα θεοῦ λαβόντες ἐν
ἑνότητι ᾄδητε ἐν φωνῇ μιᾷ διὰ Ἰησοῦ Χριστοῦ τῷ πατρὶ,
ἵνα ὑμῶν καὶ ἀκούσῃ καὶ ἐπιγινώσκῃ, δι᾿ ὧν εὖ πράσσετε,
μέλη ὄντας τοῦ υἱοῦ αὐτοῦ. χρήσιμον οὖν ἐστὶν, ὑμᾶς
ἐν ἀμώμῳ ἑνότητι εἶναι, ἵνα καὶ θεοῦ πάντοτε μετέχητε.

Εἰ γὰρ ἐγὼ ἐν μικρῷ χρόνῳ τοιαύτην συνήθειαν ἔσχον
πρὸς τὸν ἐπίσκοπον ὑμῶν, οὐκ ἀνθρωπίνην οὖσαν, ἀλλὰ
πνευματικήν, πόσῳ μᾶλλον ὑμᾶς μακαρίζω, τοὺς ἐνκεκρα-
μένους οὕτως, ὡς ἡ ἐκκλησία Ἰησοῦ Χριστῷ, καὶ ὡς Ἰησοῦς
Χριστὸς τῷ πατρὶ, ἵνα πάντα ἐν ἑνότητι σύμφωνα ᾖ;
μηδεὶς πλανάσθω· ἐὰν μή τις ᾖ ἐντὸς τοῦ θυσιαστηρίου,
ὑστερεῖται τοῦ ἄρτου τοῦ θεοῦ. εἰ γὰρ ἑνὸς καὶ δευτέρου
προσευχὴ τοσαύτην ἰσχὺν ἔχει, πόσῳ μᾶλλον ἥ τε τοῦ
ἐπισκόπου καὶ πάσης τῆς ἐκκλησίας; ὁ οὖν μὴ ἐρχό-
μενος ἐπὶ τὸ αὐτὸ, οὗτος ἤδη ὑπερηφανεῖ καὶ ἑαυτὸν διέκρι-
νεν. γέγραπται γάρ· Ὑπερηφάνοις ὁ θεὸς ἀντιτάσσεται.
σπουδάσωμεν οὖν μὴ ἀντιτάσσεσθαι τῷ ἐπισκόπῳ, ἵνα
ὦμεν θεῷ ὑποτασσόμενοι.

Ephes. xx.

Μάλιστα ἐὰν ὁ κύριός μοι ἀποκαλύψῃ, ὅτι οἱ κατ᾿
ἄνδρα κοινῇ πάντες ἐν χάριτι ἐξ ὀνόματος συνέρχεσθε ἐν
μιᾷ πίστει καὶ ἐν Ἰησοῦ Χριστῷ, τῷ κατὰ σάρκα ἐκ γένους
Δαυὶδ, τῷ υἱῷ ἀνθρώπου καὶ υἱῷ θεοῦ, εἰς τὸ ὑπακούειν
ὑμᾶς τῷ ἐπισκόπῳ καὶ τῷ πρεσβυτερίῳ ἀπερισπάστῳ δια-
νοίᾳ, ἕνα ἄρτον κλῶντες, ὅς ἐστιν φάρμακον ἀθανασίας,
ἀντίδοτος τοῦ μὴ ἀποθανεῖν, ἀλλὰ ζῆν ἐν Ἰησοῦ Χριστῷ
διὰ παντός.

Magnes. ii–iv.

Ἐπεὶ οὖν ἠξιώθην ἰδεῖν ὑμᾶς διὰ Δαμᾶ τοῦ ἀξιοθέου
ὑμῶν ἐπισκόπου καὶ πρεσβυτέρων ἀξίων Βάσσου καὶ Ἀπολ-
λωνίου καὶ τοῦ συνδούλου μου διακόνου Ζωτίωνος, οὗ ἐγὼ
ὀναίμην, ὅτι ὑποτάσσεται τῷ ἐπισκόπῳ ὡς χάριτι θεοῦ, καὶ
τῷ πρεσβυτερίῳ ὡς νόμῳ Ἰησοῦ Χριστοῦ.

Καὶ ὑμῖν δὲ πρέπει μὴ συγχρᾶσθαι τῇ ἡλικίᾳ τοῦ ἐπισκόπου, ἀλλὰ κατὰ δύναμιν θεοῦ πατρὸς πᾶσαν ἐντροπὴν

αὐτῷ ἀπονέμειν, καθὼς ἔγνων καὶ τοὺς ἁγίους πρεσβυτέρους
οὐ προσειληφότας τὴν φαινομένην νεωτερικὴν τάξιν, ἀλλ'
ὡς φρονίμους ἐν θεῷ συγχωροῦντας αὐτῷ, οὐκ αὐτῷ δέ,
ἀλλὰ τῷ πατρὶ Ἰησοῦ Χριστοῦ, τῷ πάντων ἐπισκόπῳ.
εἰς τιμὴν οὖν ἐκείνου τοῦ θελήσαντος ἡμᾶς, πρέπον ἐστὶν
ἐπακούειν κατὰ μηδεμίαν ὑπόκρισιν· ἐπεὶ οὐχ ὅτι τὸν ἐπίσκοπον τοῦτον τὸν βλεπόμενον πλανᾷ τις, ἀλλὰ τὸν ἀόρατον
παραλογίζεται. τὸ δὲ τοιοῦτον οὐ πρὸς σάρκα ὁ λόγος,
ἀλλὰ πρὸς θεόν, τὸν τὰ κρύφια εἰδότα.

Πρέπον οὖν ἐστίν, μὴ μόνον καλεῖσθαι Χριστιανούς,
ἀλλὰ καὶ εἶναι· ὥσπερ καί τινες ᾽πίσκοπον μὲν καλοῦσιν,
χωρὶς δὲ αὐτοῦ πάντα πράσσουσιν. οἱ τοιοῦτοι δὲ οὐκ
εὐσυνείδητοί μοι εἶναι φαίνονται, διὰ τὸ μὴ βεβαίως κατ'
ἐντολὴν συναθροίζεσθαι.

Magnes. vi–vii.

Ἐπεὶ οὖν ἐν τοῖς προγεγραμμένοις προσώποις τὸ πᾶν
πλῆθος ἐθεώρησα ἐν πίστει καὶ ἠγάπησα, παραινῶ, ἐν
ὁμονοίᾳ θεοῦ σπουδάζετε πάντα πράσσειν, προκαθημένου
τοῦ ἐπισκόπου εἰς τόπον θεοῦ καὶ τῶν πρεσβυτέρων εἰς
τόπον συνεδρίου τῶν ἀποστόλων, καὶ τῶν διακόνων, τῶν
ἐμοὶ γλυκυτάτων, πεπιστευμένων διακονίαν Ἰησοῦ Χριστοῦ, ὃς πρὸ αἰώνων παρὰ πατρὶ ἦν καὶ ἐν τέλει ἐφάνη.
πάντες οὖν, ὁμοήθειαν θεοῦ λαβόντες, ἐντρέπεσθε ἀλλήλους, καὶ μηδεὶς κατὰ σάρκα βλεπέτω τὸν πλησίον, ἀλλ'
ἐν Ἰησοῦ Χριστῷ ἀλλήλους διὰ παντὸς ἀγαπᾶτε. μηδὲν
ἔστω ἐν ὑμῖν, ὃ δυνήσεται ὑμᾶς μερίσαι, ἀλλ' ἑνώθητε τῷ
ἐπισκόπῳ καὶ τοῖς προκαθημένοις εἰς τύπον καὶ διδαχὴν
ἀφθαρσίας.

Ὥσπερ οὖν ὁ κύριος ἄνευ τοῦ πατρὸς οὐδὲν ἐποίησεν,
ἡνωμένος ὤν, οὔτε δι' ἑαυτοῦ, οὔτε διὰ τῶν ἀποστόλων·
οὕτως μηδὲ ὑμεῖς ἄνευ τοῦ ἐπισκόπου καὶ τῶν πρεσβυτέρων
μηδὲν πράσσετε· μηδὲ πειράσητε εὔλογόν τι φαίνεσθαι
ἰδίᾳ ὑμῖν, ἀλλ' ἐπὶ τὸ αὐτὸ μία προσευχή, μία δέησις,
εἷς νοῦς, μία ἐλπὶς ἐν ἀγάπῃ, ἐν τῇ χαρᾷ τῇ ἀμώμῳ, ὅ
ἐστιν Ἰησοῦς Χριστός, οὗ ἄμεινον οὐδὲν ἐστιν. πάντες
ὡς εἰς ἕνα ναὸν συντρέχετε θεοῦ, ὡς ἐπὶ ἓν θυσιαστήριον,

ἐπὶ ἕνα Ἰησοῦν Χριστόν, τὸν ἀφ᾽ ἑνὸς πατρὸς προελθόντα
καὶ εἰς ἕνα ὄντα καὶ χωρήσαντα.

Magnes. xiii.

Σπουδάζετε οὖν βεβαιωθῆναι ἐν τοῖς δόγμασιν τοῦ
κυρίου καὶ τῶν ἀποστόλων, ἵνα πάντα, ὅσα ποιεῖτε, κατευο-
δωθῆτε σαρκὶ καὶ πνεύματι, πίστει καὶ ἀγάπῃ, ἐν υἱῷ καὶ
πατρὶ καὶ ἐν πνεύματι, ἐν ἀρχῇ καὶ ἐν τέλει, μετὰ τοῦ
ἀξιοπρεπεστάτου ἐπισκόπου ὑμῶν καὶ ἀξιοπλόκου πνευ-
ματικοῦ στεφάνου τοῦ πρεσβυτερίου ἱμῶν καὶ τῶν κατὰ
θεὸν διακόνων. ὑποτάγητε τῷ ἐπισκόπῳ καὶ ἀλλήλοις,
ὡς Ἰησοῦς Χριστὸς τῷ πατρὶ κατὰ σάρκα, καὶ οἱ ἀπόστολοι
τῷ Χριστῷ καὶ τῷ πατρὶ καὶ τῷ πνεύματι· ἵνα ἕνωσις ᾖ
σαρκική τε καὶ πνευματική.

Trall. ii–iii.

Ὅταν γὰρ τῷ ἐπισκόπῳ ὑποτάσσησθε ὡς Ἰησοῦ Χριστῷ,
φαίνεσθέ μοι οὐ κατὰ ἄνθρωπον ζῶντες, ἀλλὰ κατὰ Ἰησοῦν
Χριστόν, τὸν δι᾽ ἡμᾶς ἀποθανόντα, ἵνα πιστεύσαντες εἰς τὸν
θάνατον αὐτοῦ τὸ ἀποθανεῖν ἐκφύγητε. ἀναγκαῖον οὖν
ἐστιν, ὥσπερ ποιεῖτε, ἄνευ τοῖ ἐπισκόπου μηδὲν πράσσειν
ὑμᾶς, ἀλλ᾽ ὑποτάσσεσθε καὶ τῷ πρεσβυτερίῳ, ὡς τοῖς
ἀποστόλοις Ἰησοῦ Χριστοῦ, τῆς ἐλπίδος ἡμῶν, ἐν ᾧ διάγον-
τες εὑρεθησόμεθα. δεῖ δὲ καὶ τοὺς διακόνους ὄντας μυ-
στηρίων Ἰησοῦ Χριστοῦ κατὰ πάντα τρόπον πᾶσιν ἀρέσκειν.
οὐ γὰρ βρωμάτων καὶ ποτῶν εἰσὶν διάκονοι, ἀλλ᾽ ἐκκλησίας
θεοῦ ὑπηρέται. δέον οὖν αὐτοὺς φυλάσσεσθαι τὰ ἐγκλή-
ματα ὡς πῦρ.

Ὁμοίως πάντες ἐντρεπέσθωσαν τοὺς διακόνους ὡς Ἰησοῦν
Χριστόν, ὡς καὶ τὸν ἐπίσκοπον, ὄντα τύπον τοῦ πατρός,
τοὺς δὲ πρεσβυτέρους ὡς συνέδριον θεοῦ καὶ ὡς σύνδεσμον
ἀποστόλων. χωρὶς τούτων ἐκκλησία οὐ καλεῖται. περὶ
ὧν πέπεισμαι ὑμᾶς οὕτως ἔχειν. τὸ γὰρ ἐξεμπλάριον τῆς
ἀγάπης ὑμῶν ἔλαβον καὶ ἔχω μεθ᾽ ἑαυτοῦ ἐν τῷ ἐπισκόπῳ
ὑμῶν, οὗ αὐτὸ τὸ κατάστημα μεγάλη μαθητεία, ἡ δὲ πραότης
αὐτοῦ δύναμις· ὃν λογίζομαι καὶ τοὺς ἀθέους ἐντρέπεσθαι.
ἀγαπῶν ὑμᾶς φείδομαι, συντονώτερον δυνάμενος γράφειν

ὑπὲρ τούτου· οὐκ εἰς τοῦτο ᾠήθην, ἵνα ὢν κατάκριτος ὡς
ἀπόστολος ὑμῖν διατάσσομαι.

Trall. vi–vii.

Παρακαλῶ οὖν ὑμᾶς, οὐκ ἐγώ, ἀλλ᾽ ἡ ἀγάπη Ἰησοῦ Χριστοῦ, μόνῃ τῇ χριστιανῇ τροφῇ χρῆσθαι, ἀλλοτρίας δὲ
βοτάνης ἀπέχεσθαι, ἥτις ἐστὶν αἵρεσις. οἱ ἑαυτοῖς παρεμ-
πλέκουσιν Ἰησοῦν Χριστὸν καταξιοπιστευόμενοι, ὥσπερ
θανάσιμον φάρμακον διδόντες μετὰ οἰνομέλιτος, ὅπερ ὁ
ἀγνοῶν ἡδέως λαμβάνει ἐν ἡδονῇ κακῇ τὸ ἀποθανεῖν.
Φυλάττεσθε οὖν τοὺς τοιούτους. τοῦτο δὲ ἔσται ὑμῖν
μὴ φυσιουμένοις, καὶ οὖσιν ἀχωρίστοις θεοῦ Ἰησοῦ Χριστοῦ καὶ τοῦ ἐπισκόπου καὶ τῶν διαταγμάτων τῶν ἀποστόλων.
ὁ ἐντὸς θυσιαστηρίου ὢν καθαρός ἐστιν· ὁ δὲ ἐκτὸς θυσιαστηρίου ὢν οὐ καθαρός ἐστιν· τοῦτ᾽ ἐστιν, ὁ χωρὶς ἐπισκόπου
καὶ πρεσβυτερίου καὶ διακόνων πράσσων τι, οὗτος οὐ
καθαρός ἐστιν τῇ συνειδήσει.

Trall. xiii.

Ἔρρωσθε ἐν Ἰησοῦ Χριστῷ, ὑποτασσόμενοι τῷ ἐπισκόπῳ
ὡς τῇ ἐντολῇ, ὁμοίως καὶ τῷ πρεσβυτερίῳ· καὶ οἱ κατ᾽
ἄνδρα ἀλλήλους ἀγαπᾶτε ἐν ἀμερίστῳ καρδίᾳ.

Rom. iv.

Οὐχ ὡς Πέτρος καὶ Παῦλος διατάσσομαι ὑμῖν. ἐκεῖνοι
ἀπόστολοι, ἐγὼ κατάκριτος· ἐκεῖνοι ἐλεύθεροι, ἐγὼ δὲ μέχρι
νῦν δοῦλος.

Rom. ix.

Μνημονεύετε ἐν τῇ προσευχῇ ὑμῶν τῆς ἐν Συρίᾳ ἐκκλησίας, ἥτις ἀντὶ ἐμοῦ ποιμένι τῷ θεῷ χρῆται. μόνος αὐτὴν
Ἰησοῦς Χριστὸς ἐπισκοπήσει, καὶ ἡ ὑμῶν ἀγάπη.

Philadelph. Inscr.

Μάλιστα ἐὰν ἐν ἑνὶ ὦσιν σὺν τῷ ἐπισκόπῳ καὶ τοῖς σὺν
αὐτῷ πρεσβυτέροις καὶ διακόνοις, ἀποδεδειγμένοις ἐν γνώμῃ
Ἰησοῦ Χριστοῦ.

Philadelph. i.

Ὃν ἐπίσκοπον ἔγνων οὐκ ἀφ' ἑαυτοῦ οὐδὲ δι' ἀνθρώπων
κεκτῆσθαι τὴν διακονίαν τὴν εἰς τὸ κοινὸν ἀνήκουσαν οὐδὲ
κατὰ κενοδοξίαν, ἀλλ' ἐν ἀγάπῃ θεοῦ πατρὸς καὶ κυρίου
Ἰησοῦ Χριστοῦ.

Philadelph. ii–iv.

Τέκνα οὖν φωτὸς ἀληθείας, φεύγετε τὸν μερισμὸν καὶ τὰς
κακοδιδασκαλίας· ὅπου δὲ ὁ ποιμήν ἐστιν, ἐκεῖ ὡς πρόβατα
ἀκολουθεῖτε.   πολλοὶ γὰρ λύκοι ἀξιόπιστοι ἡδονῇ κακῇ
αἰχμαλωτίζουσιν τοὺς θεοδρόμους· ἀλλ' ἐν τῇ ἑνότητι
ὑμῶν οὐκ ἕξουσιν τόπον.
Ἀπέχεσθε τῶν κακῶν βοτανῶν, ἅστινας οὐ γεωργεῖ
Ἰησοῦς Χριστός, διὰ τὸ μὴ εἶναι αὐτοὺς φυτείαν πατρός·
οὐχ ὅτι παρ' ὑμῖν μερισμὸν εὗρον, ἀλλ' ἀποδιϋλισμόν.
ὅσοι γὰρ θεοῦ εἰσιν καὶ Ἰησοῦ Χριστοῦ, οὗτοι μετὰ τοῦ
ἐπισκόπου εἰσίν· καὶ ὅσοι ἂν μετανοήσαντες ἔλθωσιν ἐπὶ
τὴν ἑνότητα τῆς ἐκκλησίας, καὶ οὗτοι θεοῦ ἔσονται, ἵνα
ὦσιν κατὰ Ἰησοῦν Χριστὸν ζῶντες.   μὴ πλανᾶσθε, ἀδελ-
φοί μου· εἴ τις σχίζοντι ἀκολουθεῖ, βασιλείαν θεοῦ οὐ
κληρονομεῖ· εἴ τις ἐν ἀλλοτρίᾳ γνώμῃ περιπατεῖ, οὗτος
τῷ πάθει οὐ συγκατατίθεται.
Σπουδάσατε οὖν μιᾷ εὐχαριστίᾳ χρῆσθαι· μία γὰρ σὰρξ
τοῦ κυρίου ἡμῶν Ἰησοῦ Χριστοῦ, καὶ ἓν ποτήριον εἰς ἕνωσιν
τοῦ αἵματος αὐτοῦ· ἓν θυσιαστήριον, ὡς εἷς ἐπίσκοπος ἅμα
τῷ πρεσβυτερίῳ καὶ διακόνοις, τοῖς συνδούλοις μου· ἵνα,
ὃ ἐὰν πράσσητε, κατὰ θεὸν πράσσητε.

Philadelph. vii–viii.

Ἐκραύγασα μεταξὺ ὢν, ἐλάλουν μεγάλῃ φωνῇ, θεοῦ φωνῇ·
Τῷ ἐπισκόπῳ προσέχετε καὶ τῷ πρεσβυτερίῳ καὶ διακόνοις·
οἱ δὲ ὑποπτεύσαντές με ὡς προειδότα τὸν μερισμόν τινων
λέγειν ταῦτα· μάρτυς δέ μοι, ἐν ᾧ δέδεμαι, ὅτι ἀπὸ σαρκὸς
ἀνθρωπίνης οὐκ ἔγνων.   τὸ δὲ πνεῦμα ἐκήρυσσεν, λέγον
τάδε· Χωρὶς τοῦ ἐπισκόπου μηδὲν ποιεῖτε· τὴν σάρκα ὑμῶν
ὡς ναὸν θεοῦ τηρεῖτε· τὴν ἕνωσιν ἀγαπᾶτε, τοὺς μερισμοὺς

φεύγετε· μιμηταὶ γίνεσθε Ἰησοῦ Χριστοῦ, ὡς καὶ αὐτὸς τοῦ πατρὸς αὐτοῦ.

Ἐγὼ μὲν οὖν τὸ ἴδιον ἐποίουν, ὡς ἄνθρωπος εἰς ἕνωσιν κατηρτισμένος. οὗ δὲ μερισμός ἐστιν καὶ ὀργὴ, θεὸς οὐ κατοικεῖ. πᾶσιν οὖν μετανοοῦσιν ἀφίει ὁ κύριος, ἐὰν μετανοήσωσιν εἰς ἑνότητα θεοῦ καὶ συνέδριον τοῦ ἐπισκόπου. πιστεύω τῇ χάριτι Ἰησοῦ Χριστοῦ, ὃς λύσει ἀφ᾽ ὑμῶν πάντα δεσμόν. παρακαλῶ δὲ ὑμᾶς, μηδὲν κατ᾽ ἐρίθειαν πράσσειν, ἀλλὰ κατὰ χριστομαθίαν·

Smyrn. viii–ix.

Πάντες τῷ ἐπισκόπῳ ἀκολουθεῖτε, ὡς Ἰησοῦς Χριστὸς τῷ πατρί, καὶ τῷ πρεσβυτερίῳ ὡς τοῖς ἀποστόλοις· τοὺς δὲ διακόνους ἐντρέπεσθε, ὡς θεοῦ ἐντολήν. μηδεὶς χωρὶς τοῦ ἐπισκόπου τι πρασσέτω τῶν ἀνηκόντων εἰς τὴν ἐκκλησίαν. ἐκείνη βεβαία εὐχαριστία ἡγείσθω, ἡ ὑπὸ ἐπίσκοπον οὖσα, ἢ ᾧ ἂν αὐτὸς ἐπιτρέψῃ. ὅπου ἂν φανῇ ὁ ἐπίσκοπος, ἐκεῖ τὸ πλῆθος ἔστω· ὥσπερ ὅπου ἂν ᾖ Χριστὸς Ἰησοῦς, ἐκεῖ ἡ καθολικὴ ἐκκλησία. οὐκ ἐξόν ἐστιν χωρὶς τοῦ ἐπισκόπου οὔτε βαπτίζειν οὔτε ἀγάπην ποιεῖν· ἀλλ᾽ ὃ ἂν ἐκεῖνος δοκιμάσῃ, τοῦτο καὶ τῷ θεῷ εὐάρεστον, ἵνα ἀσφαλὲς ᾖ καὶ βέβαιον πᾶν ὃ πράσσεται.

Εὔλογόν ἐστιν λοιπὸν ἀνανῆψαι καὶ, ὡς ἔτι καιρὸν ἔχομεν, εἰς θεὸν μετανοεῖν. καλῶς ἔχει, θεὸν καὶ ἐπίσκοπον εἰδέναι. ὁ τιμῶν ἐπίσκοπον ὑπὸ θεοῦ τετίμηται· ὁ λάθρα ἐπισκόπου τι πράσσων τῷ διαβόλῳ λατρεύει.

Polycarp. iv.

Μηδὲν ἄνευ γνώμης σου γινέσθω, μηδὲ σὺ ἄνευ θεοῦ τι πρᾶσσε· ὅπερ οὐδὲ πράσσεις.

Polycarp. v.

Ἐὰν καυχήσηται, ἀπώλετο· καὶ ἐὰν γνωσθῇ πλέον τοῦ ἐπισκόπου, ἔφθαρται. πρέπει δὲ τοῖς γαμοῦσι καὶ ταῖς γαμουμέναις μετὰ γνώμης τοῦ ἐπισκόπου τὴν ἕνωσιν ποιεῖσθαι, ἵνα ὁ γάμος ᾖ κατὰ κύριον, καὶ μὴ κατ᾽ ἐπιθυμίαν.

APPENDIX II

THE SCHEME OF ST. CYPRIAN

§. 1. *The Treatise De Vnitate.*

A FULL account of St. Cyprian's doctrine of the Church has to be gathered from the whole of his writings, and especially from the sixty-two Letters which illustrate the activity of his short episcopate. The chief features of it, however, and most of the characteristic terms employed, are found in the treatise *De Catholicae Ecclesiae Vnitate*, written at the time when Confessors of the Decian persecution were vexing the Church of Carthage with their factious conduct, and leading a revolt against his authority. I set down here the most important sections, placing side by side the alternative texts of the fourth chapter. The text is that of Hartel in C.S.E.L.

THASCI CAECILI CYPRIANI DE CATHOLICAE ECCLESIAE VNITATE, CC. 3–14

3. Cauenda sunt autem non solum quae sunt aperta adque manifesta sed et astutae fraudis subtilitate fallentia. quid uero astutius quidue subtilius, quam

ut Christi aduentu detectus ac prostratus inimicus,
postquam lux gentibus uenit et sospitandis hominibus
salutare lumen effulsit, ut surdi auditum gratiae
spiritalis admitterent, aperirent ad Dominum oculos
caeci, infirmi aeterna sanitate reualescerent, clodi ad
ecclesiam currerent, muti claris uocibus et precibus
orarent, uidens ille idola derelicta et per nimium
credentium populum sedes suas et templa deserta
excogitauerit nouam fraudem, ut sub ipso christiani
nominis titulo fallat incautos? haereses inuenit et
schismata, quibus subuerteret fidem, ueritatem cor-
rumperet, scinderet unitatem. quos detinere non
potest in uiae ueteris caecitate circumscribit et decipit
noui itineris errore. rapit de ipsa ecclesia homines
et, dum sibi adpropinquasse iam lumini adque euasisse
saeculi noctem uidentur, alias nescientibus tenebras
rursus infundit, ut cum euangelio Christi et cum
obseruatione eius et lege non stantes christianos se
uocent et ambulantes in tenebris habere se lumen
existiment blandiente aduersario adque fallente, qui
secundum apostoli uocem transfigurat se uelut ange-
lum lucis et ministros subornat suos uelut ministros
iustitiae adserentes noctem pro die, interitum pro
salute, desperationem sub obtentu spei, perfidiam sub
praetexto fidei, antichristum sub uocabulo Christi,
ut dum uerisimilia mentiuntur, ueritatem subtilitate
frustrentur. hoc eo fit, fratres dilectissimi, dum ad
ueritatis originem non reditur nec caput quaeritur nec
magisterii caelestiis doctrina seruatur.

4. Quae si quis consideret et examinet, tractatu
longo adque argumentis opus non est. probatio
est ad fidem facilis conpendio ueritatis. loquitur
Dominus ad Petrum: ego tibi dico, inquit, quia
tu es Petrus et super istam petram aedificabo ecclesiam meam, et portae inferorum non uincent eam.
dabo tibi claues regni caelorum: et quae ligaueris

z

super terram erunt ligata et in caelis, et quaecum-que solueris super terram erunt soluta et in caelis.

et idem post resurrectionem suam dicit : pasce oues meas. super unum aedificat ecclesiam et illi pascendas oues mandat suas, et quamuis apostolis omnibus parem tribuat potestatem, unam tamen cathedram constituit et unitatis originem adque rationem sua¹ auctoritate disposuit. hoc erant utique et ceteri quod Petrus, sed primatus Petro datur ut una ecclesia et cathedra una monstretur. et pastores sunt omnes, sed grex unus ostenditur, qui ab apostolis omnibus unanimi consensione pascatur. hanc et Pauli unitatem qui non tenet, tenere se fidem credit? qui cathedram Petri super quam fundata ecclesia est deserit, in ecclesia se esse confidit?

super unum aedificat ecclesiam, et quamuis apostolis omnibus post resurrectionem suam parem potestatem tribuat et dicat: sicut misit me pater et ego mitto uos. accipite Spiritum sanctum: si cuius remiseritis peccata, remittentur illi: si cuius tenueritis, tenebuntur, tamen ut unitatem manifestaret, unitatis eiusdem originem ab uno incipientem sua auctoritate disposuit. hoc erant utique et ceteri apostoli quod fuit Petrus, pari consortio praediti et honoris et potestatis, sed exordium ab unitate proficiscitur, ut ecclesia Christi una monstretur. quam unam ecclesiam etiam in cantico canticorum Spiritus sanctus ex persona Domini designat et dicit: una est columba mea, perfecta mea, una est matri suae, electa genetrici suae. hanc ecclesiae unitatem qui non tenet tenere se fidem credit? qui ecclesiae renititur et resistit in ecclesia se esse confidit?

¹ *Codd.* atque orationis suae, *sed manu secunda* atque *deletum est.*

quando et beatus apostolus Paulus hoc idem doceat
et sacramentum unitatis ostendat dicens : unum corpus et unus spiritus, una spes uocationis uestrae, unus
Dominus, una fides, unum baptisma, unus Deus.

5. Quam unitatem tenere firmiter et uindicare debemus, maxime episcopi qui in ecclesia praesidemus, ut
episcopatum quoque ipsum unum adque indiuisum
probemus. nemo fraternitatem mendacio fallat, nemo
fidem ueritatis perfida praeuaricatione corrumpat.
episcopatus unus est, cuius a singulis in solidum
pars tenetur. ecclesia una est quae in multitudinem
latius incremento fecunditatis extenditur, quomodo
solis multi radii sed lumen unum, et rami arboris
multi sed robur unum tenaci radice fundatum, et cum
de fonte uno riui plurimi defluunt, numerositas licet
diffusa uideatur exundantis copiae largitate, unitas
tamen seruatur in origine. auelle radium solis a corpore, diuisionem lucis unitas non capit : ab arbore
frange ramum, fractus germinare non poterit : a fonte
praecide riuum, praecisus arescit. sit et ecclesia
Domini luce perfusa per orbem totum radios suos
porrigit : unum tamen lumen est quod ubique diffun-
ditur, nec unitas corporis separatur. ramos suos in
uniuersam terram copia ubertatis extendit, profluentes
largiter riuos latius pandit : unum tamen caput est
et origo una et una mater fecunditatis successibus
copiosa : illius fetu nascimur, illius lacte nutrimur,
spiritu eius animamur.

6. Adulterari non potest sponsa Christi, incorrupta
est et pudica. unam domum nouit, unius cubiculi
sanctitatem casto pudore custodit. haec nos Deo
seruat, haec filios regno quos generauit adsignat.
quisque ab ecclesia segregatus adulterae iungitur a
promissis ecclesiae separatur, nec perueniet ad Christi
praemia qui reliquit ecclesiam Christi. alienus est,
profanus est, hostis est. habere non potest Deum

patrem qui ecclesiam non habet matrem. si potuit
euadere quisque extra arcam Noe fuit, et qui extra
ecclesiam foris fuerit euadit. monet Dominus et dicit :
qui non est mecum aduersus me est, et qui non
mecum colligit spargit. qui pacem Christi et concordiam rumpit aduersus Christum facit : qui alibi
praeter ecclesiam colligit Christi ecclesiam spargit.
dicit Dominus : ego et pater unum sumus. et iterum
de Patre et Filio et Spiritu sancto scriptum est : et
tres unum sunt. et quisquam credit hanc unitatem
de diuina firmitate uenientem, sacramentis caelestibus
cohaerentem scindi in ecclesia posse et uoluntatum
conlidentium diuortio separari ? hanc unitatem qui
non tenet, non tenet Dei legem, non tenet Patris et
Filii fidem, uitam non tenet et salutem.

7. Hoc unitatis sacramentum, hoc uinculum concordiae inseparabiliter cohaerentis ostenditur, quando in
euangelio tunica Domini Iesu Christi non diuiditur
omnino nec scinditur, sed sortientibus de ueste
Christi, quis Christum potius indueret, integra uestis
accipitur et incorrupta adque indiuidua tunica possi-
detur. loquitur ac dicit scriptura diuina : de tunica
autem, quia de superiore parte non consutilis sed per
totum textilis fuerat, dixerunt ad inuicem : non scin-
damus illam sed sortiamur de ea, cuius sit. unitatem
ille portabat de superiore parte uenientem id est de
caelo et a patre uenientem quae ab accipiente ac
possidente scindi omnino non poterat, sed totam
semel et solidam firmitatem inseparabiliter obtinebat.
possidere non potest indumentum Christi qui scindit
et diuidit ecclesiam Christi. contra denique cum
Salomone moriente regnum eius et populus scindere-
tur, Achias propheta Hieroboam regi obuius factus
in campo in duodecim scissuras uestimentum suum
discidit dicens : sume tibi decem scissuras, quia haec
dicit Dominus : ecce scindo regnum de manu Salo-

monis et dabo tibi decem sceptra, et duo sceptra
erunt ei propter seruum meum Dauid et propter
Hierusalem ciuitatem quam elegi, ut ponam nomen
meum illic. cum duodecim tribus Israel scinderentur,
uestimentum suum propheta Achias discidit. at uero
quia Christi populus non potest scindi, tunica eius
per totum textilis et cohaerens diuisa a possidentibus
non est : indiuidua, copulata, conexa ostendit populi
nostri qui Christum induimus concordiam cohaerentem. sacramento uestis et signo declarauit ecclesiae
unitatem.

* * * * *

10. Hinc haereses et factae sunt frequenter et fiunt,
dum peruersa mens non habet pacem, dum perfidia
discordans non tenet unitatem. fieri uero haec Dominus permittit et patitur manente propriae libertatis
arbitrio, ut dum corda et mentes nostras ueritatis
discrimen examinat, probatorum fides integra manifesta luce clarescat. per apostolum praemonet Spiritus
sanctus et dicit : oportet et haereses esse, ut probati
manifesti sint in uobis, sic probantur fideles, sic per-
fidi deteguntur, sic et ante iudicii diem hic quoque
iam iustorum adque iniustorum animae diuiduntur et
a frumento paleae separantur. hinc sunt qui se ultro
aput temerarios conuenas sine diuina dispositione
praeficiunt, qui se praepositos sine ulla ordinationis
lege constituunt, qui nemine episcopatum dante episcopi sibi nomen adsumunt : quos designat in psalmis
Spiritus sanctus sedentes in pestilentiae cathedra,
pestes et lues fidei, serpentis ore fallentes et corrum-
pendae ueritatis artifices, uenena letalia linguis pesti-
feris euomentes : quorum sermo ut cancer serpit,
quorum tractatus pectoribus et cordibus singulorum
mortale uirus infundit.

11. Contra eiusmodo clamat Dominus, ab his re-
frenat et reuocat errantem plebem suam dicens : nolite

audire sermones pseudoprophetarum,quoniam uisiones
cordis eorum frustrantur eos. locuntur sed non ab ore
Domini. dicunt eis qui abiciunt uerbum Dei : pax
erit uobis et omnibus ambulantibus in uoluntatibus
suis, omnis qui ambulat errore cordis sui non uenient
super te mala. non locutus sum ad eos, et ipsi pro-
phetauerunt. si stetissent in substantia mea et audis-
sent uerba mea et si docuissent populum meum,
conuertissem eos a malis cogitationibus eorum. hos
eosdem denuo Dominus designat et denotat dicens:
me dereliquerunt fontem aquae uitae et effoderunt
sibi lacus detritos qui non possunt aquam portare.
quando aliud baptisma praeter unum esse non possit,
baptizare se opinantur : uitae fonte deserto uitalis et
salutaris aquae gratiam pollicentur. non abluuntur
illic homines sed potius sordidantur, nec purgantur
delicta sed immo cumulantur. non Deo natiuitas illa
sed diabolo filios generat. per mendacium nati ueritatis promissa non capiunt : de perfidia procreati fidei
gratiam perdunt. ad pacis praemium uenire non possunt qui pacem Domini discordiae furore ruperunt.

12. Nec se quidam uana interpretatione decipiant,
quod dixerit Dominus: ubicumque fuerint duo aut tres
collecti in nomine meo, ego cum eis sum. corruptores
euangelii adque interpretes falsi extrema ponunt et
superiora praetereunt, partis memores et partem sub-
dole conprimentes : ut ipsi ab ecclesia scissi sunt, ita
capituli unius sententiam scindunt. Dominus enim
cum discipulis suis unanimitatem suaderet et pacem :
dico, inquit, uobis quoniam si duobus ex uobis conuenerit in terra, de omni re, quamcumque petieritis,
continget uobis a patre meo qui in caelis est. ubicumque enim fuerint duo aut tres collecti in nomine
meo, ego cum eis sum, ostendens non multitudini sed
unanimitati deprecantium plurimum tribui. si duobus,
inquit, ex uobis conuenerit in terra : unanimitatem

prius posuit, concordiam pacis ante praemisit : ut
conueniat nobis, fideliter et firmiter docuit. quomodo
autem potest ei cum aliquo conuenire, cui cum corpore ipsius ecclesiae et cum uniuersa fraternitate non
conuenit ? quomodo possunt duo aut tres in nomine
Christi colligi quos constet a Christo et ab eius euangelio separari ? non enim nos ab illis, sed illi a nobis
recesserunt et cum haereses et schismata postmodum
nata sint, dum conuenticula sibi diuersa constituunt,
ueritatis caput adque originem reliquerunt. Dominus
autem de ecclesia sua loquitur et ad hos qui sunt in
ecclesia loquitur, ut si ipsi concordes fuerint, ut secundum quod mandauit et monuit duo aut tres licet
collecti unanimiter orauerint, duo aut tres licet sint,
inpetrare possint de Dei maiestate quod postulant.
ubicumque fuerint duo aut tres, ego, inquit, cum eis
sum, cum simplicibus scilicet adque pacatis, cum
Deum timentibus et Dei praecepta seruantibus. cum
his duobus uel tribus licet esse se dixit, quomodo et
cum tribus pueris in camino ignis fuit et quia in
Deum simplices adque inter se unanimes permane-
bant, flammis ambientibus medios spiritu roris anima-
uit, quomodo apostolis duobus in custodia clausis,
quia simplices, quia unanimes erant, ipse adfuit, ipse
resolutis carceris claustris, ut uerbum quod fideliter
praedicabant multitudini traderent, ad forum rursus
inposuit. quando ergo in praeceptis suis ponit et
dicit : ubi fuerint duo aut tres, ego cum eis sum, non
homines ab ecclesia diuidit qui instituit et fecit ecclesiam, sed exprobrans discordiam perfidis et fidelibus
pacem sua uoce commendans ostendit magis esse se
cum duobus aut tribus unanimiter orantibus quam
cum dissidentibus plurimis plusque inpetrari posse
paucorum concordi prece quam discordiosa oratione
multorum.

13. Ideo et cum orandi legem daret, addidit dicens :

et cum steteritis ad orationem, remittite si quid habetis
aduersus aliquem, ut et pater uester qui in caelis est
remittat peccata uobis. et ad sacrificium cum dissensione uenientem reuocat ab altari et iubet prius con-
cordare cum fratre, tunc cum pace redeuntem Deo
munus offerre, quia nec ad Cain munera respexit
Deus : neque enim habere pacatum Deum poterat
qui cum fratre pacem per zeli discordiam non habe-
bat. quam sibi igitur pacem promittunt inimici fratrum ? quae sacrificia celebrare se credunt aemuli
sacerdotum ? secum esse Christum, cum collecti
fuerint, opinantur qui extra Christi ecclesiam col-
liguntur ?

14. Tales etiam si occisi in confessione nominis
fuerint, macula ista nec sanguine abluitur : inexpiabilis
et grauis culpa discordiae nec passione purgatur. esse
martyr non potest qui in ecclesia non est : ad regnum
peruenire non poterit qui eam quae regnatura est
dereliquit. pacem nobis Christus dedit, concordes
adque unanimes esse praecepit, dilectionis et caritatis
foedera incorrupta adque inuiolata mandauit : exhi-
bere se non potest martyrem qui fraternam non tenuit
caritatem. docet hoc et contestatur Paulus apostolus
dicens : et si habuero fidem ita ut montes transferam,
caritatem autem non habeam, nihil sum : et si in
cibos distribuero omnia mea et si tradidero corpus
meum ut ardeam, caritatem autem non habeam, nihil
proficio. caritas magnanima est, caritas benigna est,
caritas non aemulatur, non inflatur, non inritatur,
non agit perperam, non cogitat malum, omnia diligit,
omnia credit, omnia sperat, omnia sustinet. caritas
numquam excidet. numquam, inquit, excidet caritas.
haec enim semper in regno erit, haec in aeternum
fraternitatis sibi cohaerentis unitate durabit. ad
regnum caelorum non potest peruenire discordia, ad
praemium Christi qui dixit : hoc est mandatum meum

ut diligatis inuicem, quemadmodum dilexi uos, per-
tinere non poterit qui dilectionem Christi perfida
dissensione uiolauit. qui caritatem non habet Deum
non habet. Iohannis beati apostoli uox est: Deus,
inquit, dilectio est et qui manet In dilectione in Deo
manet et Deus in illo manet. cum Deo manere non
possunt qui esse in ecclesia Dei unanimes noluerunt.
ardeant licet flammis et ignibus traditi uel obiecti
bestiis animas suas ponant, non erit illa fidei corona
sed poena perfidiae nec religiosae uirtutis exitus
gloriosus sed desperationis interitus. occidi talis potest, coronari non potest. sic se christianum esse
profitetur, quomodo et Christum diabolus saepe men-
titur ipso Domino praemonente et dicente: multi
uenient in nomine meo dicentes: ego sum Christus,
et multos fallent. sicut ille Christus non est, quamuis
fallat in nomine, ita nec christianus uideri potest qui
non permanet in euangelio eius et fidei ueritate.

§ 2. *The Alternative Texts.*

In an Appendix to my lectures on *Catholicity*,
published in 1914 but written at an earlier
date, I stated my conviction that the alternative texts of chapter four, which I have
here placed side by side, are both from the
hand of St. Cyprian. I was not aware at the
time that I had been anticipated in this respect
by Dom John Chapman ; intent on my own
study of the text, I had neglected recent
writings on the subject—a lamentable confession—and so had missed the advantages to
be derived from his articles in the *Revue*

Bénédictine, vol. xix and xx. It is now time
to acknowledge his priority. The evidence
can be summarily stated as follows.

Two manuscripts of the eighth or ninth
century (marked by Hartel as Q and M),
which are obviously derived from the same
archetype, contain both texts, the second (with
the variant of *aedificauit* for *aedificat*) following
immediately upon the first. Other MSS. of
this or earlier date contain the second text
only. Others, again, give various conflations
of the two texts. The first text is quoted,
though without reference to St. Cyprian, in
a homily of the Ven. Bede (P.L. xciv. 218).
A conflated text is quoted as Cyprian's about
A.D. 585 by Pelagius II (*Ep.* iv, P.L. lxxii.
913). This shows that conflations were already
current. The internal evidence is equally good
for the two texts, both showing the characteristics of the writer. The conclusion seems
to be imperative that St. Cyprian issued the
treatise on two separate occasions with this
variation, and possibly some other minor variations of the text.

I differ from Dom John Chapman in thinking that the text which I have placed first had
the priority, and that St. Cyprian afterwards

substituted the second. The considerations which impel me to this conclusion are two :—

1. The words *hanc et Pauli unitatem* in the first text lead naturally to the subsequent words *quando et beatus apostolus Paulus*, which follow with extreme abruptness upon the second text.[1]

2. A sufficient cause can be found, as I will presently show, for the suppression of the first text by St. Cyprian, and the substitution of the second. No good cause is shown for the reverse process. The suggestion that the first text was substituted when the treatise, originally designed to meet troubles at Carthage, was afterwards sent to Rome on the occasion of the Novatian schism, rests on the supposition that the phrase *cathedra Petri* looks to the particular circumstances of that Church. But St. Cyprian does not so use it.

§ 3. *Cathedra Petri*

This point is of some importance, because on it turns St. Cyprian's theory of the equality of bishops. The term *cathedra Petri* does not occur in Christian literature before his time,

---

[1] I cannot think that Dom John Chapman is right in reading with some of the conflated MSS. *hanc Petri unitatem* or *hanc ecclesiae unitatem* (*Revue Bénédictine*, xix. 370). *Hanc et Pauli* is certainly the *lectio difficilior* ; the others are obvious substitutes, one of them being derived from the second text.

but there are indications of use unlike his.
When Tertullian spoke of the *cathedrae apostolorum* as continuing in the Churches of express
apostolic foundation,[1] it is obvious that a
cathedra Petri might be sought at Antioch or
at Rome, both Churches claiming St. Peter as
founder. That, however, is not St. Cyprian's
use. In *De Vnitate* 4 the *cathedra Petri* is
clearly identical with the *una cathedra*. But
the *una cathedra*, as the whole argument
demands, is unquestionably the bishop's seat
of authority in each several Church, the seat of
the "episcopatus unus adque indiuisus." Dom
John Chapman allows this, adding the remark
that at Rome this seat was the seat of Peter.[2]
But to press that is to spoil the argument
about the *una cathedra* and the *primatus* of
Peter. The indivisible apostolic and episcopal
authority holds the Church in one ; this is
exactly what was given to Peter (*parem potestatem tribuat . . . hoc erant et ceteri*), and the
first place was given to him singly for the
purpose of demonstrating that unity. Thus
episcopal authority, wherever constituted, is
designated by the term *cathedra Petri*. The
whole argument then coheres ; to be in the

[1] *De Praescr.* 36.   [2] *The Catholic Encyclopaedia, s.v.* Cyprian.

Church is to be with the bishop, he who separates himself from the bishop "cathedram Petri deserit."[1]

Compare these passages.

(*a*) Cyprian addresses Rogatianus, whose deacon was defying him :—

Cum pro episcopatus uigore et cathedrae auctoritate haberes potestatem qua posses de illo statim uindicari. —*Ep*. iii. 1.

(*b*) He speaks of the faction of Felicissimus at Carthage, and of his own authority as bishop :—

Deus unus est et Christus unus et una ecclesia et cathedra una super Petrum Domini uoce fundata. aliud altare constitui aut sacerdotium nouum fieri praeter unum altare et unum sacerdotium non potest. —*Ep*. xliii. 5.

(*c*) He says that Cornelius was duly promoted bishop at Rome—

cum Fabiani locus id est cum locus Petri et gradus cathedrae sacerdotalis uacaret.—*Ep*. lv. 8.

(*d*) He writes of Novatian, making a faction at Rome :—

Qui episcopo Cornelio in catholica ecclesia de Dei iudicio et cleri ac plebis suffragio ordinato profanum

---

[1] Cf. *Ep*. lxvi. 8 : Scire debes episcopum in ecclesia esse et ecclesiam in episcopo et si qui cum episcopo non sit in ecclesia non esse.

altare erigere et adulteram cathedram conlocare et
sacrilega contra uerum sacerdotem sacrificia offerre
temptauerit.—*Ep.* lxviii. 2.

It is clear that the *cathedra una* is the same
alike at Nova, at Carthage, and at Rome, that
in each case alike it is *cathedra Petri* or *super
Petrum fundata*, that Felicissimus and Novatian
stand in exactly the same relation to it, as also
Cyprian and Cornelius. This seems to leave
no room for doubting that in *De Vnitate* 4, as
the context implies, *cathedra Petri* is a synonym
for the episcopate.

But is this use of the phrase found anywhere
else ? When I was previously writing on the
subject I could find no evidence except an
obscure reference in a sermon, probably Gallic,
erroneously attributed to St. Augustine ;[1] but
my friend Mr. J. Arthur Price, of Lincoln's
Inn, has recently called my attention to the
Increpatio in Clerum of Gildas (P.L. lxix. 367),
who inveighs fiercely against the simoniacal
bishops of his time in Britain :—

c. i. Sedem Petri apostoli immundis pedibus aliquos
usurpantes, sed merito cupiditatis in Iudae traditoris
pestilentem cathedram desidentes.

c. ii. Iudam quodam modo in Petri cathedram

[1] *Catholicity*, p. 130.

Domini traditorem, et Nicolaum immundae haereseos
adiutorem in loco Stephani martyris statuunt.

   c. xxiv. Petro eiusque successoribus dicit Dominus :
Et tibi dabo claues regni caelorum : uobis uero : Non
noui uos ; discedite a me operarii iniquitatis.

With these he contrasts others "qui apostolicam sedem legitime obtinent." It is clear
that Gildas (*saec.* vi) regarded every bishop as
occupying an apostolic see, which was expressly
cathedra Petri. We may either trace in this the
influence of St. Cyprian or find in it evidence
that he was not altogether singular in his use
of the phrase.

It remains to examine a much-quoted passage in St. Cyprian's letter to Cornelius about
the appeal of the faction of Felicissimus to
Rome :—

Quibus etiam satis non fuit ab euangelio recessisse,
spem lapsis satisfactionis et paenitentiae sustulisse,
fraudibus inuolutos uel adulteriis commaculatos uel
sacrificiorum funesta contagione pollutos, ne Deum
rogarent, ne in ecclesia exomologesin criminum
facerent, ab omni et sensu et fructu paenitentiae
remouisse, foris sibi extra ecclesiam et contra
ecclesiam constituisse conuenticulum perditae fac-
tionis, quo male sibi consciorum et Deum rogare
ac satisfacere nolentium caterua conflueret: post
ista adhuc insuper pseudoepiscopo sibi ab haereticis
constituto nauigare audent et ad Petri cathedram
adque ad ecclesiam principalem unde unitas sacerdotalis exorta est ab schismaticis et profanis lit-

teras ferre nec cogitare eos esse Romanos quorum
fides apostolo praedicante laudata est, ad quos perfidia habere non possit accessum. quae autem causa
ueniendi et pseudoepiscopum contra episcopos factum nuntiandi? aut enim placet illis quod fecerunt
et in suo scelere perseuerant: aut si displicet et
recedunt, sciunt quo reuertantur. nam cum statutum
sit ab omnibus nobis et aequum sit pariter ac iustum
ut uniuscuiusque causa illic audiatur ubi est crimen
admissum, et singulis pastoribus portio gregis sit
adscripta quam regat unusquisque et gubernet
rationem sui actus Domino redditurus, oportet utique
eos quibus praesumus non circumcursare nec episcoporum concordiam cohaerentem sua subdola et fallaci
temeritate conlidere, sed agere illic causam suam ubi
et accusatores habere et testes sui criminis possint:
nisi si paucis desperatis et perditis minor uidetur esse
auctoritas episcoporum in Africa constitutorum, qui
de illis iam iudicauerunt et eorum conscientiam multis
delictorum laqueis uinctam iudicii sui nuper grauitate
damnarunt. iam causa eorum cognita est, iam de eis
dicta sententia est, nec censurae congruit sacerdotum
mobilis adque inconstantis animi leuitate reprehendi,
cum Dominus doceat et dicat: sit sermo uester, est
est, non non.—*Ep.* lviiii. 14.

If the words "ad Petri cathedram adque ad
ecclesiam principalem unde unitas sacerdotalis
exorta est" be Cyprian's own a great part of
my argument fails.   I have given in the second
lecture my reasons for concluding that they
are not his, but are rather a quotation from
the letter "ab schismaticis et profanis" which
the appellants carried with them—a justifica-

tion, in fact, of their appeal.   The words "nisi si paucis desperatis, etc.," seem to strike directly at the expression "ecclesia principalis." Cyprian's own conception of the source "unde unitas sacerdotalis exorta est" may be gathered from *De Vnitate*, with which compare his words addressed to Iubaianus during his quarrel with Stephen of Rome :—

Nam Petro primum Dominus, super quem aedificauit ecclesiam et unde unitatis originem instituit et osten-dit, potestatem istam dedit ut id solueretur [in terris] quod ille soluisset.—*Ep.* lxxiii. 7.

"Unitas exorta est" from Peter at Caesarea Philippi, not from Peter at Rome.

§ 4.   *The Revision of the Text.*

Here I find the sufficient cause for the sup-pression of the first text of *De Vnitate* 4, and the substitution of the second.   The schismatics at Carthage appealed to Rome as specifically *Petri cathedra*.   Moreover it is clear from Firmilian's angry letter that Stephen was shortly afterwards pressing this use of the term :—

Atque ego in hac parte iuste indignor ad hanc tam apertam et manifestam Stephani stultitiam, quod qui sic de episcopatus sui loco gloriatur et se successionem Petri tenere contendit, super quem fundamenta eccle-siae collocata sunt, multas alias petras inducat et ecclesiarum multarum noua aedificia constituat, dum esse illic baptisma sua auctoritate defendit. nam qui baptizantur complent sine dubio ecclesiae numerum : qui autem baptisma eorum probat, de baptizatis et ecclesiam illic esse confirmat. nec intellegit offuscari a se et quodam modo aboleri christianae petrae ueritatem qui sic prodit et deserit unitatem. Iudaeos tamen quamuis ignorantia caecos et grauissimo facinore constrictos zelum Dei apostolus habere profitetur. Stephanus qui per successionem cathedram Petri habere se praedicat nullo aduersus haereticos zelo excitatur, etc.—*Ep*. lxxv. 17.

With this compare Cyprian's own words to Quintus on the same subject :—

Nam nec Petrus quem primum Dominus elegit et super quem aedificauit ecclesiam suam, cum secum Paulus de circumcisione postmodum disceptaret, uindicauit sibi aliquid insolenter aut adroganter adsumpsit, ut diceret se primatum tenere et obtemperari a nouellis et posteris sibi potius oportere.—*Ep*. lxxi. 3.

The words *primatus* and *Petri cathedra* being thus brought into controversial use against him, in a sense which he repudiated, it is not surprising that he should have recast the passage of his treatise in which they occurred, striking out the misused words and laying additional emphasis on the complete equality of the Apostles and the bishops their successors. He could allow that Rome " pro magnitudine sua " might take precedence of Carthage (*Ep*.

lii. 2), but he made that grudging admission, perhaps with some subtlety, only by way of accounting for the greater mischief done by Nouatus in the larger city. Spiritually he and Cornelius were equals, "pari consortio praediti et honoris et potestatis."

§ 5. The Authority of Synods.

The authority of a group of "coepiscopi" over a single bishop is rather implied than expressed in the writings of St. Cyprian, who does not seem to have worked out any theory of conciliar action. It is implied in the obligation "ut episcopatum quoque ipsum unum adque indiuisum probemus." For this forbids eccentric conduct on the part of any one bishop ; he must conform to the judgement of his peers. Anything like a formal condemnation or deposition seems, indeed, to be excluded by the emphatic words of St. Cyprian in the Council *de Haereticis Baptizandis* :—

Neque enim quisquam nostrum episcopum se episcoporum constituit aut tyrannico terrore ad obsequendi necessitatem collegas suos adigit. quando habeat omnis episcopus pro licentia libertatis et potestatis suae arbitrium proprium tamque iudicari ab alio non possit, quam nec ipse possit alterum iudicare. sed expectemus uniuersi iudicium

Domini nostri Iesu Christi qui unus et solus habet
potestatem et praeponendi nos in ecclesiae suae guber-
natione et de actu nostro iudicandi.—*Hartel*, p. 436.

But this consists with the action of " coepiscopi " or " consacerdotes " in the promotion of
a bishop, as witness the *locus classicus* about
Cornelius :—

Factus est episcopus a plurimis collegis nostris qui
tunc in urbe Roma aderant, qui ad nos litteras
honorificas et laudabiles et testimonio suae praedica-
tionis inlustres de eius ordinatione miserunt. factus
est autem Cornelius episcopus de Dei et Christi eius
iudicio, de clericorum paene omnium testimonio, de
plebis quae tunc adfuit suffragio, de sacerdotum
antiquorum et bonorum uirorum collegio.—*Ep.* lv. 8.

In regard to the removal of a bishop the
position is more obscure. He sometimes speaks
as if nothing could justify separation from a
duly appointed pastor :—

Neque enim aliunde haereses obortae sunt aut nata
sunt schismata *quam* quando sacerdoti Dei non obtem-
peratur nec unus in ecclesia ad tempus sacerdos et
ad tempus iudex uice Christi cogitatur : cui si secundum magisteria diuina obtemperaret fraternitas
uniuersa, nemo aduersum sacerdotum collegium
quicquam moueret, nemo post diuinum iudicium, post
populi suffragium, post coepiscoporum consensum,
iudicem se non iam episcopis sed Deo faceret, etc.—
Ep. lviiii. 5.

Yet, writing of Novatian, he says that even
if he had been duly promoted bishop his

schismatical conduct would have deprived him
of that character :—

Episcopatum autem tenere non posset, etiam si
episcopus prius factus a coepiscoporum suorum corpore et ab ecclesiae unitate desciscerет, quando apostolus admoneat ut inuicem nosmet ipsos sustineamus,
ne ab unitate quam Deus constituit recedamus, et
dicat : sustinentes inuicem in dilectione, satis agentes
seruare unitatem spiritus in coniunctione pacis. qui
ergo nec unitatem spiritus nec coniunctionem pacis
obseruat et se ab ecclesiae uinculo adque a sacerdotum
collegio separat, episcopi nec potestatem potest habere
nec honorem qui episcopatus nec unitatem uoluit
tenere nec pacem.—*Ep*. lv. 24.

Dealing with the case of Basilides and Mar-
tial, he and a council of African bishops say
roundly that the faithful ought to withdraw
from an unfaithful pastor :—

Nec sibi plebs blandiatur quasi inmunis esse a
contagio delicti possit cum sacerdote peccatore com-
municans et ad iniustum adque inlicitum praepositi
sui episcopatum consensum suum commodans . . .
propter quod plebs obsequens praeceptis dominicis et
Deum metuens a peccatore praeposito separare se
debet, nec se ad sacrilegi sacerdotis sacrificia miscere,
quando ipsa maxime habeat potestatem uel eligendi
dignos sacerdotes uel indignos recusandi.—*Ep*. lxvii. 3.

The idea seems to be that as the consent of
the faithful is required for the promotion of a
bishop, so they have power to depose him.
But this would make them his judges, which

was certainly not according to the mind of St. Cyprian and his colleagues. Behind this apparent inconsistency there probably lies a conviction that the manifest offences which could alone justify such action were themselves evidence of a divine judgement already given against the offender. Moreover, the exclusion of the defaulting bishop became definitive only when a successor was duly appointed, and this implied a judgement of his case by the bishops concurring in the appointment. Sabinus was duly appointed to succeed Basilides, and the African bishops, interpreting this as a *iudicium*, condemned the attempt of Basilides to obtain reinstation through the intervention of Stephen of Rome :—

Propter quod diligenter de traditione diuina et apostolica obseruatione seruandum est et tenendum quos apud nos quoque et fere per prouincias uniuersas tenetur, ut ad ordinationes rite celebrandas ad eam plebem cui praepositus ordinatur episcopi eiusdem prouinciae proximi quique conueniant et episcopus deligatur plebe praesente, quae singulorum uitam plenissime nouit et uniuscuiusque actum de eius conuersatione perspexit. quod et apud uos factum uidemus in Sabini collegae nostri ordinatione, ut de uniuersae fraternitatis suffragio et de episcoporum qui in praesentia conuenerant quique de eo ad uos [1] litteras fecerant iudicio episcopatus ei deferretur et

[1] *Legendum fortasse* nos.

manus ei in locum Basilidis inponeretur. nec rescin-
dere ordinationem iure perfectam potest quod Basilides
post crimina sua detecta et conscientiae etiam propriae
confessione nudata Romam pergens Stephanum col-
legam nostrum longe positum et gestae rei ac ueritatis
ignarum fefellit, ut exambiret reponi se iniuste in
episcopatum de quo fuerat iure depositus.—*Ibid.* 5.

Soon afterwards Cyprian himself was urging
Stephen to intervene in the affairs of Gaul.
Marcian of Arles had joined with the following
of Novatian, and was refusing to admit the
lapsed to penance. It would seem that nobody
in the neighbourhood was willing to act ;
Cyprian therefore begged Stephen to take the
lead :—

Dirigantur in prouinciam et ad plebem Arelate
consistentem a te litterae quibus abstento Marciano
alius in loco eius substituatur et grex Christi qui in
hodiernum ab illo dissipatus et uulneratus contemnitur
colligatur. sufficiat multos illic ex fratribus nostris
annis istis superioribus excessisse sine pace. uel
ceteris subueniatur qui supersunt et diebus ac noc-
tibus ingemescunt et diuinam ac paternam miseri-
cordiam deprecantes solacium nostrae opitulationis
exposcunt. idcirco enim, frater carissime, copiosum
corpus est sacerdotum concordiae mutuae glutino
atque unitatis uinculo copulatum, ut si quis ex collegio nostro haeresim facere et gregem Christi lacerare
et uastare temptauerit, subueniant ceteri, qua pastores
utiles et misericordes oues dominicas in gregem col-
ligant.

*　*　*　*　*

Nam etsi pastores multi sumus, unum tamen gregem pascimus, et oues universas quas Christus sanguine suo et passione quaesiuit colligere et fouere debemus nec pati supplices et dolentes fratres nostros crudeliter despici et superba quorundam praesumptione calcari.

* * * * *

Ex quibus cum Marcianus esse coeperit et se Nouatiano coniungens aduersarius misericordiae et pietatis extiterit, sententiam non dicat, sed accipiat, nec sic agat quasi ipse iudicauerit de collegio sacerdotum, quando ipse sit ab uniuersis sacerdotibus iudicatus.—*Ep.* lxviii. 3, 4.

It is evident how confused was the practice, and how great was the need of a regular conciliar system under the leadership of the principal sees.

§ 6.   *The Nature of Schism.*

From the passages quoted above St. Cyprian's conception of schism can be sufficiently gathered. According to him schism does not divide the Church, which is essentially indivisible ; but schismatics pass altogether outside the Church. In the case of internal schism he is quite clear, "si qui cum episcopo non sit in ecclesia non esse." The case of external schism is not quite as clear, but his treatment of Novatian— on the hypothesis of his having been legitimately promoted to the episcopate—and of Marcian

leaves little room for doubt that, in his judgement, a bishop breaking away from the fellowship of his *consacerdotes* would equally pass out
of the Church.

In that event he would lose all capacity to
act as a bishop : " episcopi nec potestatem
potest habere nec honorem." For Cyprian
could not think of any spiritual endowments
of the Church as existing outside the Church.
That is the sole ground of his rejection of the
baptism of heretics and schismatics ; such an
one is *foris constitutus*, and has nothing of that
kind to give :—

Neque enim potest pars illic inanis esse et pars
praeualere. si baptizare potuit, potuit et spiritum
sanctum dare. si autem sanctum spiritum dare non
potest, quia foris constitutus cum sancto spiritu non
est, nec baptizare uenientem potest, quando et
baptisma unum sit et spiritus sanctus unus et una
ecclesia a Christo Domino nostro super Petrum
origine unitatis et ratione fundata. ita fit ut cum
omnia apud illos inania et falsa sint, nihil eorum
quod illi gesserint probari a nobis debeat. quid
enim potest ratum et firmum esse apud Dominum
quod illi faciunt quos Dominus hostes et aduersarios
suos dicit in euangelio suo ponens: qui non est
mecum aduersus me est : et qui non mecum colligit,
spargit ; et beatus quoque apostolus Iohannes mandata Domini et praecepta custodiens in epistula sua
posuerit : audistis quia antichristus uenit. nunc
autem antichristi multi facti sunt. unde cognosci-

mus quia nouissima hora est.   ex nobis exierunt,
sed non fuerunt ex nobis.   si enim fuissent ex nobis,
mansissent nobiscum.   unde nos quoque colligere
et considerare debemus an qui aduersarii sunt Domini
et appellati sunt antichristi possint dare gratiam
Christi.—*Ep.* lxx. 3.

It will be observed that St. Cyprian treated
all schismatics alike as antichristian; he did
not distinguish between heresy or schism and
apostasy.   In this respect, and in his teaching
about the emptiness of the sacraments administered by schismatics, he was closely followed
by the Donatists.   The contrary opinion, which
became prevalent in the Catholic Church, was
stated as against them by Optatus.   In a rather
heavy bantering style he insisted on giving
Parmenianus the title of "frater," protesting
that they were born of one mother Church,
isdem sacramentorum uisceribus, and were proved
by their common use of the Lord's Prayer to
be sons of one Father.   He drew the conclusion, in spite of his vehement condemnation
of schism, that schismatics are not entirely
(*in totum*) separated from Catholics.   In view
of my last lecture the whole passage is worth
quoting :—

Huius rei apertissimam ueritatem, Parmeniane
frater, agnosce.   si tamen hoc nomen fraternitatis

frequenter a me dictum libenter audire dignaris,
fac ut tibi sit fastidiosum, tamen nobis est necessarium, ne forte iuxta probationem huius nominis
tacendo rei esse uideamur. si enim tu non uis esse
frater, ego incipio inpius, si de nomine isto tacuero.
estis enim fratres nostri et nos uestri propheta dicente:
nonne nos unus deus creauit et unus pater genuit?
non enim potestis non esse fratres, cum omnibus
dictum sit: dii estis et filii altissimi omnes. et nos
et uos unum praeceptum accepimus, in quo dictum
est: ne uocetis uobis quemquam patrem in terris,
quia unus est pater uester in caelis. saluator noster
Christus solus natus est filius dei; sed et nos et uos
filii dei uno modo facti sumus, sicut in euangelio
scriptum est: uenit filius dei: quotquot eum rece-
perunt, dedit eis potestatem, ut filii dei fierent, qui
credunt in nomine eius. nos et facti sumus et
dicimur, uos et facti estis et non dicimini, quia
pacifici esse non uultis nec audire ipsum filium
dei dicentem: felices pacifici, quia ipsi filii dei
uocabuntur. Christus ueniens deum et hominem
reuocauit in pacem: et fecit ambos unum tollens
medium saepem parietis. uos nobiscum, id est
cum fratribus, pacem habere non uultis. non enim
potestis non esse fratres, quos isdem sacramentorum
uisceribus una mater ecclesia genuit, quos eodem
modo adoptiuos filios deus pater excepit. unde
huius temporis praescius Christus, quia futurum
erat, ut a nobis hodie discordaretis, talia dedit orandi
mandata, ut uel in oratione unitas remansisset, ut
iungerent preces, quos discrepaturae fuerunt partes.
oramus pro uobis, quia uolumus, et uos pro nobis,
et cum non uultis. aut dicat unus quisque uestrum:
"pater meus, qui in caelis es," et "panem meum
cotidianum da mihi hodie," et "dimitte mihi peccata,
quomodo et ego debitori meo." igitur si quae man-

data sunt, mutari non possunt, uidetis nos non in
totum ab inuicem esse separatos, dum et nos pro
uobis oramus uolentes et uos pro nobis oratis etsi
nolentes.   uides, frater Parmeniane, sanctae ger-
manitatis uincula inter uos et uos in totum rumpi
non posse.—*Lib*. iv, *c*. 2.

APPENDIX III

THE PROVINCIAL SYNOD OF CANTERBURY, A.D. 1606

THE Provincial Synod of Canterbury, assembled in the year 1603 and continued by adjournments and prorogations to the year 1610, adopted a long series of dogmatic chapters setting out the principles of spiritual and temporal government, to most of which formal constitutions or canons were appended. Owing to the opposition of the King, James I, who took alarm at the doctrine of the legitimacy of all temporal governments established *de facto* plainly expressed in them, these canons were never promulgated. What degree of authority the argumentative chapters may have is not clear, but there can be no doubt that the canons represent the formal judgement of the sacred synod. I have extracted one of them to show the official treatment of the episcopal theory by the Church of England. The text is taken from the volume published in 1690,

under the title, "Bishop Overall's Convocation-
Book, MDCVI, Concerning the Government of GOD's Catholick Church and the
Kingdoms of the Whole World," and reprinted
in the Library of Anglo-Catholic Theology,
A.D. 1844. A note in Cosin's handwriting
establishes the fact that the canons belong to
the session of the year 1606.

Provincial Synod of Canterbury, A.D. 1606.

Book II.   Canon VII.

And therefore if any man shall affirm, under colour
of any thing that is in the Scriptures, either that the
inscriptions or directions of the second epistle of
St. Paul to Timothy, or of his epistle to Titus,
though they are found in the ancient copies of the
Greek Testament, are of no credit or authority; or,
that such an impeachment and discredit laid upon
them is not very prejudicial to the books and writings
of the Holy Ghost; or, that it is not great presumption for men in these days to take upon them to know
better whether Timothy and Titus were bishops,
than the churches and godly Fathers did, which were
planted and lived either in the Apostles' times or
presently after them, except they have some especial
revelations from God; or, that whilst men do labour to
bring into discredit the ancient Fathers and primitive
churches, they do not derogate from themselves such
credit as they hunt after, and as much as in them
lieth bring many parts of religion unto a wonderful
uncertainty; or, that it is probable, or was possible
for Timothy to have observed those rules that St. Paul
gave him until the coming of Christ, except, as the

Fathers expound some of them, he meant to have them first observed by himself and other bishops in that age, and that afterwards they should so likewise be observed by all bishops for ever ; or, that the ancient Fathers and ecclesiastical histories, when they record it to all posterity, that these men, and those men, were made by the Apostles bishops of such and such places, are not to be held to be of more credit than any other historiographers or writers ; or, that when the ancient Fathers did collect out of the Scriptures and practice of the Apostles the continuance for ever of that form of church-government which was then in use, they were not so throughly illuminated with the Holy Ghost as divers men of late have been ; or, that it was an idle course held by the primitive churches and ancient Fathers, to keep the catalogues of their bishops, or to ground arguments in some cases upon their succession, in that they were able to deduce their beginnings either from the Apostles or from some apostolical persons ; or, that the form of government used in the Apostles' times, for the planting and ordering of churches, was not, in many respects, as necessary to be continued in the Church afterwards; especially considering that many churches were not left fully ordered, nor in some places were at all planted, when the Apostles died ; or, that true and perfect order, grounded upon the very laws of nature and reason, and established by the Holy Ghost in the Apostles' times, was not fit for the churches of God afterwards to embrace and observe ; or, that any church, since the Apostles' times, till of late, when it received the Gospel, had not likewise bishops and archbishops for the government of it ; or, that divers of the ancient Fathers did not hold, and that very truly, for aught that appeareth to the contrary, that our Saviour Christ and His Apostles, in establishing the form of church-government amongst the Gentiles, had an especial respect to that form which God had settled amongst the Jews, and did no way purpose to abrogate or abolish it; or, that any since the Apostles' times, till of late days, was ever held to be a lawful minister of the Word and Sacraments, who was not ordained priest or minister by the imposition of the hands of some bishop; or, that it is with any probability to be imagined that all the churches of Christ and ancient Fathers from the beginning would ever have held it for an apostolical rule that none but bishops had any authority to make priests, had they not thought and judged that the same authority had been derived unto them, the said bishops, from the same apostolical ordination that it was committed unto Timothy and Titus, their predecessors; or, that the Apostles and all the ancient Fathers were deceived when they judged the authority of bishops necessary at all times for the suppressing of schisms; and that without bishops there would be in the churches as many sects as ministers; or, that when men find themselves, in regard of their disobedience to their bishops, so fully and notably described and censured by all the ancient Fathers for schismatics and contentious persons, they have not just cause to fear their own estates, if they continue in such their wilfulness and obstinacy; or, that the church-government, by us above treated of, is truly to be said to savour of Judaism, more than the observation by godly kings and princes of the equity of the judicial law given to the Jews, may truly be said to savour thereof; or, that it doth proceed from any other than the wicked spirit, for any sort of men, what godly show soever they can pretend, to seek to discredit, as much as in them lieth, that form of church-government which was

established by the Apostles, and left by them to
continue in the Church to the end of the world, under
archbishops and bishops, such as were Timothy and
Titus, and some others, then called to those offices
by the said Apostles, and ever since held by the
primitive churches and all the ancient Fathers to
be apostolical functions ; or, to term the same or any
part of it to be anti-Christian, he doth greatly err.

APPENDIX IV

THE CONSTITUTION *PASTOR AETERNUS*

FOR convenient reference I here append the dogmatic decree of the Vatican Council *De Ecclesia*. The text is printed from Denzinger's *Enchiridion Symbolorum et Definitionum*.

Concilium Vaticanum, A.D. 1870.

Sessio IV.

Constitutio I. de Ecclesia Christi.

Pastor aeternus et episcopus animarum nostrarum, ut salutiferum redemptionis opus perenne redderet, sanctam aedificare Ecclesiam decrevit, in qua veluti in Domo Dei viventis fideles omnes unius fidei et charitatis vinculo continerentur. Quapropter, priusquam clarificaretur, rogavit Patrem non pro Apostolis tantum, sed et pro eis, qui credituri erant per verbum eorum in ipsum, ut omnes unum essent, sicut ipse Filius et Pater unum sunt. Quemadmodum igitur Apostolos, quos sibi de mundo elegerat, misit, sicut ipse missus erat a Patre : ita in Ecclesia sua Pastores et Doctores usque ad consummationen saeculi esse voluit. Ut vero episcopatus ipse unus et indivisus esset, et per cohaerentes sibi invicem sacerdotes credentium multitudo universa in fidei et communionis

unitate conservaretur, beatum Petrum caeteris Apostolis praeponens in ipso instituit perpetuum utriusque
unitatis principium ac visibile fundamentum, super
cujus fortitudinem aeternum exstrueretur templum,
et Ecclesiae coelo inferenda sublimitas in hujus fidei
firmitate consurgeret. Et quoniam portae inferi ad
evertendam, si fieri posset, Ecclesiam, contra ejus
fundamentum divinitus positum majori in dies odio
undique insurgunt; Nos ad catholici gregis custo-
diam, incolumitatem, augmentum, necessarium esse
judicamus, sacro approbante Concilio, doctrinam de
institutione, perpetuitate, ac natura sacri Apostolici
primatus, in quo totius Ecclesiae vis ac soliditas
consistit, cunctis fidelibus credendam et tenendam,
secundum antiquam atque constantem universalis
Ecclesiae fidem, proponere, atque contrarios, domi-
nico gregi adeo perniciosos, errores proscribere et
condemnare.

Cap. i. De Apostolici Primatus in beato Petro institutione.

Docemus itaque et declaramus, juxta Evangelii
testimonia primatum jurisdictionis in universam Dei
Ecclesiam immediate et directe beato Petro Apostolo
promissum atque collatum a Christo Domino fuisse.
Unum enim Simonem, cui jam pridem dixerat: Tu
vocaberis Cephas, postquam ille suam edidit con-
fessionem inquiens: Tu es Christus, Filius Dei vivi,
solemnibus his verbis allocutus est Dominus: Beatus
es, Simon Bar-Jona, quia caro et sanguis non reve-
lavit tibi, sed Pater meus, qui in coelis est: et ego
dico tibi, quia tu es Petrus, et super hanc Petram
aedificabo Ecclesiam meam, et portae inferi non
praevalebunt adversus eam: et tibi dabo claves
regni coelorum: et quodcumque ligaveris super
terram, erit ligatum et in coelis: et quodcumque
solveris super terram, erit solutum et in coelis.

Atque uni Simoni Petro contulit Jesus post suam resurrectionem summi pastoris et rectoris jurisdictionem in totum suum ovile dicens: Pasce agnos meos: Pasce oves meas. Huic tam manifestae sacrarum Scripturarum doctrinae, ut ab Ecclesia catholica semper intellecta est, aperte opponuntur pravae eorum sententiae, qui, constitutam a Christo Domino in sua Ecclesia regiminis formam pervertentes, negant, solum Petrum prae caeteris Apostolis, sive seorsum singulis sive omnibus simul, vero proprioque jurisdictionis primatu fuisse a Christo instructum: aut qui affirmant, eundem primatum non immediate directeque ipsi beato Petro, sed Ecclesiae, et per hanc illi ut ipsius Ecclesiae ministro delatum fuisse.

Si quis igitur dixerit, beatum Petrum Apostolum non esse a Christo Domino constitutum Apostolorum omnium principem et totius Ecclesiae militantis visibile caput; vel eundem honoris tantum, non autem verae propriaeque jurisdictionis primatum ab eodem Domino nostro Jesu Christo directe et immediate accepisse; anathema sit.

Cap. 2.   De perpetuitate Primatus beati Petri in Romanis
Pontificibus.

Quod autem in beato Apostolo Petro princeps pastorum et pastor magnus ovium Dominus Christus Jesus in perpetuam salutem ac perenne bonum Ecclesiae instituit, id eodem auctore in Ecclesia, quae fundata super petram ad finem saeculorum usque firma stabit, jugiter durare necesse est. Nulli sane dubium, imo saeculis omnibus notum est, quod sanctus beatissimusque Petrus, Apostolorum princeps et caput fideique columna, et Ecclesiae catholicae fundamentum, a Domino nostro Jesu Christo, Salvatore humani generis ac Redemptore, claves regni

accepit: qui ad hoc usque tempus et semper in
suis succesoribus, episcopis sanctae Romanae Sedis,
ab ipso fundatae, ejusque consecratae sanguine, vivit
et praesidet et judicium exercet. Unde quicumque
in hac Cathedra Petro succedit, is secundum Christi
ipsius institutionem primatum Petri in universam
Ecclesiam obtinet. Manet ergo dispositio veritatis,
et beatus Petrus, in accepta fortitudine petrae per-
severans, suscepta Ecclesiae gubernacula non reliquit.
Hac de causa ad Romanam Ecclesiam propter poten-
tiorem principalitatem necesse semper fuit omnem
convenire Ecclesiam, hoc est, eos, qui sunt undique
fideles, ut in ea Sede, e qua venerandae communionis
jura in omnes dimanant, tamquam membra in capite
consociata, in unam corporis compagem coalescerent.

Si quis ergo dixerit, non esse ex ipsius Christi
Domini institutione, seu jure divino, ut beatus Petrus
in primatu super universam Ecclesiam habeat per-
petuos successores; aut Romanum Pontificem non
esse beati Petri in eodem primatu successorem;
anathema sit.

Cap. 3.   De vi et ratione Primatus Romani Pontificis.

Quapropter apertis innixi sacrarum litterarum
testimoniis, et inhaerentes tum Praedecessorum
Nostrorum, Romanorum Pontificum, tum Conciliorum generalium disertis perspicuisque decretis,
innovamus oecumenici Concilii Florentini defini-
tionem, qua credendum ab omnibus Christi fidelibus
est, sanctam Apostolicam Sedem, et Romanum
Pontificem in universum orbem tenere primatum, et
ipsum Pontificem Romanum successorem esse beati
Petri, principis Apostolorum, et verum Christi
Vicarium, totiusque Ecclesiae caput, et omnium
Christianorum patrem ac doctorem existere; et ipsi
in beato Petro pascendi, regendi ac gubernandi

universalem Ecclesiam a Domino nostro Jesu Christo
plenam potestatem traditam esse; quemadmodum
etiam in gestis oecumenicorum Conciliorum et in
sacris canonibus continetur.

Docemus proinde et declaramus, Ecclesiam Romanam, disponente Domino, super omnes alias ordinariae potestatis obtinere principatum, et hanc Romani
Pontificis jurisdictionis potestatem, quae vere episcopalis est, immediatam esse: erga quam cujuscunque
ritus et dignitatis pastores atque fideles, tam seorsum
singuli quam simul omnes, officio hierarchicae sub-
ordinationis veraeque obedientiae obstringuntur, non
solum in rebus, quae ad fidem et mores, sed etiam in
iis, quae ad disciplinam et regimen Ecclesiae per
totum orbem diffusae pertinent; ita ut, custodita cum
Romano Pontifice tam communionis, quam ejusdem
fidei professionis unitate, Ecclesia Christi sit unus
grex sub uno summo pastore. Haec est catholicae
veritatis doctrina, a qua deviare salva fide atque
salute nemo potest.

Tantum autem abest, ut haec Summi Pontificis
potestas officiat ordinariae ac immediatae illi episcopalis jurisdictionis potestati, qua Episcopi, qui positi
a Spiritu Sancto in Apostolorum locum successerunt,
tamquam veri pastores assignatos sibi greges, singuli
singulos, pascunt et regunt, ut eadem a supremo et
universali Pastore asseratur, roboretur ac vindicetur,
secundum illud sancti Gregorii Magni: Meus honor
est honor universalis Ecclesiae. Meus honor est
fratrum meorum solidus vigor. Tum ego vere
honoratus sum, cum singulis quibusque honor debitus
non negatur.

Porro ex suprema illa Romani Pontificis potestate
gubernandi universam Ecclesiam jus eidem esse
consequitur, in hujus sui muneris exercitio libere
communicandi cum pastoribus et gregibus totius

Ecclesiae, ut iidem ab ipso in via salutis doceri ac
regi possint. Quare damnamus ac reprobamus illorum
sententias, qui hanc supremi capitis cum pastoribus
et gregibus communicationem licite impediri posse
dicunt, aut eandem reddunt saeculari potestati
obnoxiam, ita ut contendant, quae ab Apostolica
Sede vel ejus auctoritate ad regimen Ecclesiae con-
stituuntur, vim ac valorem non habere, nisi potestatis
saecularis placito confirmentur.

Et quoniam divino Apostolici primatus jure
Romanus Pontifex universae Ecclesiae praeest,
docemus etiam et declaramus, eum esse judicem
supremum fidelium, et in omnibus causis ad examen
ecclesiasticum spectantibus ad ipsius posse judicium
recurri; Sedis vero Apostolicae, cujus auctoritate
major non est, judicium a nemine fore retractandum,
neque cuiquam de ejus licere judicare judicio. Quare
a recto veritatis tramite aberrant, qui affirmant, licere
ab judiciis Romanorum Pontificum ad oecumenicum
Concilium tamquam ad auctoritatem Romano Pontifice superiorem appellare.

Si quis itaque dixerit, Romanum Pontificem habere
tantummodo officium inspectionis vel directionis, non
autem plenam et supremam potestatem jurisdictionis
in universam Ecclesiam, non solum in rebus, quae
ad fidem et mores, sed etiam in iis, quae ad disciplinam
et regimen Ecclesiae per totum orbem diffusae pertinent; aut eum habere tantum potiores partes, non
vero totam plenitudinem hujus supremae potestatis;
aut hanc ejus potestatem non esse ordinariam et
immediatam sive in omnes ac singulas ecclesias, sive
in omnes et singulos pastores et fideles; anathema sit.

Cap. 4. De Romani Pontificis infallibili magisterio.

Ipso autem Apostolico primatu, quem Romanus
Pontifex, tamquam Petri principis Apostolorum

successor, in universam Ecclesiam obtinet, supremam
quoque magisterii potestatem comprehendi, haec
Sancta Sedes semper tenuit, perpetuus Ecclesiae
usus comprobat, ipsaque oecumenica Concilia, ea
imprimis, in quibus Oriens cum Occidente in fidei
charitatisque unionem conveniebat, declaraverunt.
Patres enim Concilii Constantinopolitani quarti,
majorum vestigiis inhaerentes, hanc solemnem edi-
derunt professionem : Prima salus est, rectae fidei
regulam custodire. Et quia non potest Domini
nostri Jesu Christi praetermitti sententia dicentis :
Tu es Petrus, et super hanc Petram aedificabo
Ecclesiam meam, haec, quae dicta sunt, rerum probantur effectibus, quia in Sede Apostolica immaculata
est semper catholica reservata religio, et sancta cele-
brata doctrina. Ab hujus ergo fide et doctrina
separari minime cupientes, speramus, ut in una
communione, quam Sedes Apostolica praedicat, esse
mereamur, in qua est integra et vera Christianae
religionis soliditas. Approbante vero Lugdunensi
Concilio secundo, Graeci professi sunt : Sanctam
Romanam Ecclesiam summum et plenum primatum
et principatum super universam Ecclesiam catholicam
obtinere, quem se ab ipso Domino in beato Petro,
Apostolorum principe sive vertice, cujus Romanus
Pontifex est successor, cum potestatis plenitudine
recepisse veraciter et humiliter recognoscit ; et sicut
prae caeteris tenetur fidei veritatem defendere, sic et,
si quae de fide subortae fuerint quaestiones, suo debent
judicio definiri. Florentinum denique Concilium
definivit : Pontificem Romanum, verum Christi
Vicarium, totiusque Ecclesiae cuput et omnium
Christianorum patrem ac doctorem existere ; et ipsi
in beato Petro pascendi, regendi ac gubernandi universalem Ecclesiam a Domino nostro Jesu Christo
plenam potestatem traditam esse.

Huic pastorali muneri ut satisfacerent, Praede-
cessores Nostri indefessam semper operam dederunt,
ut salutaris Christi doctrina apud omnes terrae
populos propagaretur, parique cura vigilarunt, ut,
ubi recepta esset, sincera et pura conservaretur.
Quocirca totius orbis Antistites, nunc singuli, nunc
in Synodis congregati, longam ecclesiarum consue-
tudinem et antiquae regulae formam sequentes, ea
praesertim pericula, quae in negotiis fidei emerge-
bant, ad hanc Sedem Apostolicam retulerunt, ut ibi
potissimum resarcirentur damna fidei, ubi fides non
potest sentire defectum. Romani autem Pontifices,
prout temporum et rerum conditio suadebat, nunc
convocatis oecumenicis Conciliis aut explorata Ecclesiae per orbem dispersae sententia, nunc per Synodos
particulares, nunc aliis, quae divina suppeditabat
providentia, adhibitis auxiliis, ea tenenda defini-
verunt, quae sacris Scripturis et apostolicis Traditionibus consentanea, Deo adjutore, cognoverant.
Neque enim Petri succesoribus Spiritus Sanctus
promissus est, ut eo revelante novam doctrinam
patefacerent, sed ut, eo assistente, traditam per Apostolos revelationem seu fidei depositum sancte
custodirent et fideliter exponerent. Quorum quidem
apostolicam doctrinam omnes venerabiles Patres
amplexi et sancti Doctores orthodoxi venerati atque
secuti sunt ; plenissime scientes, hanc sancti Petri
Sedem ab omni semper errore illibatam permanere.
secundum Domini Salvatoris nostri divinam pollicita-
tionem discipulorum suorum principi factam : Ego
rogavi pro te, ut non deficiat fides tua, et tu aliquando
conversus confirma fratres tuos.

Hoc igitur veritatis et fidei numquam deficientis
charisma Petro ejusque in hac Cathedra successoribus
divinitus collatum est, ut excelso suo munere in
omnium salutem fungerentur, ut universus Christi

grex per eos ab erroris venenosa esca aversus, coelestis doctrinae pabulo nutriretur, ut, sublata schismatis occasione, Ecclesia tota una conservaretur, atque suo fundamento innixa, firma adversus inferi portas consisteret.

At vero cum hac ipsa aetate, qua salutifera Apostolici muneris efficacia vel maxime requiritur, non pauci inveniantur, qui illius auctoritati obtrectant; necessarium omnino esse censemus, praerogativam, quam unigenitus Dei Filius cum summo pastorali officio conjungere dignatus est, solemniter asserere.

Itaque Nos traditioni a fidei Christianae exordio perceptae fideliter inhaerendo, ad Dei Salvatoris nostri gloriam, religionis Catholicae exaltationem et Christianorum populorum salutem, sacro approbante Concilio, docemus et divinitus revelatum dogma esse definimus : Romanum Pontificem, cum ex Cathedra loquitur, id est, cum omnium Christianorum Pastoris et Doctoris munere fungens pro suprema sua Apostolica auctoritate doctrinam de fide vel moribus ab universa Ecclesia tenendam definit, per assistentiam divinam, ipsi in beato Petro promissam, ea infallibilitate pollere, qua divinus Redemptor Ecclesiam suam in definienda doctrina de fide vel moribus instructam esse voluit ; ideoque ejusmodi Romani Pontificis definitiones ex sese, non autem ex consensu Ecclesiae, irreformabiles esse.

Si quis autem huic Nostrae definitioni contradicere, quod Deus avertat, praesumpserit; anathema sit.

APPENDIX V

THE BELGIC CONFESSION

THE doctrine of Equality of Ministers, the basis of Presbyterianism, is nowhere better expressed than in the Belgic Confession. Originally written in French, A.D. 1561, to state the principles of the Reformed in Flanders, Artois, and other provinces of the Netherlands, it was translated into Flemish and adopted by a general assembly of the Reformed of those regions in the year 1579. Three years afterwards it was published in Latin. I reproduce certain chapters of this version, which had a great influence in England and Scotland. The text is taken from the *Sylloge Confessionum*, issued from the Clarendon Press in the year 1804.

CONFESSIO BELGICA

XXVII. Credimus et confitemur unicam Ecclesiam Catholicam seu universalem. Quae est vera congregatio seu coetus omnium fidelium Christianorum, qui totam suam salutem ab uno Jesu Christo expectant, quatenus videlicet ipsius sanguine sunt

abluti, et per Spiritum ejus sanctificati atque obsig-
nati. Haec porro Ecclesia ut ab initio mundi fuit,
ita et usque ad ejus finem est perduratura. Id vel
ex eo apparet, quod Christus rex aeternus est, qui
nunquam sine subditis esse potest. Caeterum hanc
Ecclesiam Deus contra omnem mundi furorem et
impetum tuetur: quamvis ad aliquod tempus parva
admodum et quasi extincta in conspectu hominum
appareat: quemadmodum tempore illo periculosis-
simo Achabi Deus sibi septem millia virorum reser-
vasse dicitur, qui non flexerant genu coram Baal.
Denique haec Ecclesia sancta nullo est aut certo loco
sita et circumscripta, aut ullis certis ac singularibus
personis astricta aut alligata. Sed per omnem orbem
terrarum sparsa atque diffusa, quamvis animo ac
voluntate in uno eodemque spiritu, virtute fidei, tota
sit simul conjuncta atque unita.

XXVIII. Credimus quod quum sacer hic coetus
et congregatio sit eorum qui servari debent; et salus
nulla sit extra eam; neminem (cujuscunque dignitatis
aut nominis is fuerit) sese ab ea subducere aut
segregare debere, ut sua tantum consuetudine con-
tentus solus, ac separatim vivat. Sed contra omnes
ac singulos teneri huic coetui se adjungere, et Ecclesiae unitatem sollicite conservare, seseque illius tum
doctrinae tum disciplinae subjicere, collum denique
Christi jugo sponte submittere, et tanquam com-
munia ejusdem corporis membra aedificationi fratrum inservire, prout Deus unicuique sua dona fuerit
largitus. Porro ut haec melius observentur, omnium
fidelium partes sunt, sese juxta Dei verbum ab eis
omnibus disjungere, qui sunt extra Ecclesiam con-
stituti: huicque fidelium coetui ac congregationi sese
adjungere, ubicunque illam Deus constituerit: etsi id
contraria principum vel magistratuum edicta pro-
hibeant, indicta etiam in eos capitis et mortis

corporeae poena, qui id fecerint. Quicunque igitur
a vera illa Ecclesia recedunt, aut sese illi aggregare
recusant, aperte Dei mandato repugnant.

XXIX. Credimus summa tum diligentia, tum
prudentia, ex Dei verbo esse inquirendum ac discer-
nendum quaenam sit illa vera Ecclesia : quandoqui-
dem omnes sanctae,[1] quotquot hodie in mundo
vigent, Ecclesiae titulum nomenque usurpant, atque
praetexunt. Nequaquam vero de hypocritarum
coetu nunc loquimur, qui bonis in Ecclesia sunt
permisti, licet ad Ecclesiam proprie non pertineant,
in qua corpore sunt praesentes : sed de distinguendo
duntaxat verae Ecclesiae corpore ac congregatione,
ab aliis omnibus sectis, quae se Ecclesiae membra
esse falso gloriantur. His igitur notis vera Ecclesia
a falsa discernetur. Si in illa pura Evangelii prae-
dicatio, legitimaque Sacramentorum ex Christi praescripto administratio vigeat : si item recta disciplina
Ecclesiastica utatur ad coercenda vitia : si denique
(ut uno verbo cuncta complectamur) ad normam
verbi Dei omnia exigat, et quaecunque huic adver-
santur repudiet : Christumque unicum caput agnos-
cat. His, inquam, notis certum est veram Ecclesiam
dignosci posse: a qua fas non sit quenquam disjungi.
Quae autem sint verae hujus Ecclesiae vera membra,
ex communibus Christianorum omnium notis poterit
judicari : qualis est fides, qua, semel Christo ceu
unico suo Salvatore apprehenso, fugiunt peccatum,
et sequuntur justitiam : verum item Deum ac proxi-
mos suos diligunt, neque ad dextram, neque ad
sinistram deflectentes : carnem suam, cum ipsius
effectis, crucifigunt, minime id quidem quasi nulla
amplius in illis sit infirmitas : sed quod adversus
illam per omne vitae tempus virtute Spiritus pugnent,
et subinde ad sanguinem, mortem, passionemque et

[1] *Sic: legendum est fortasse* sectae.

obedientiam Christi Domini nostri, tanquam ad
tutissimum praesidium, refugiant : ut in quo solo
sciant se habere redemptionem peccatorum, per fidem
in illum.   Falsa vero Ecclesia contra sibi ipsi suis-
que institutis et traditionibus plus semper quam Dei
verbo tribuit : Christi vero jugo subjici se non
patitur : nec Sacramenta ex Christi praescripto
administrat : sed illis pro arbitrio modo addit aliquid,
modo detrahit.   Praeterea hominibus illa semper,
plus quam Christo, nititur : et eos qui sancte, ex
praescripto verbi Dei, vitam suam componere
student ; quive vitia illius, veluti avaritiam et idolo-
manias, taxant ac reprehendunt, hostiliter persequi-
tur.   Ex his igitur facile est utramque Ecclesiam ab
invicem discernere, et agnoscere.

XXX.   Credimus veram hanc Ecclesiam debere
regi, ac gubernari spirituali illa politia, quam nos
Deus ipse verbo suo edocuit : ita ut sint in ea
Pastores ac Ministri, qui pure et concionentur, et
Sacramenta administrent.   Sint quoque Seniores, et
Diaconi, qui Ecclesiae senatum constituant, ut his
veluti mediis vera religio conservari, veraque
doctrina passim retineri et propagari possit : homi-
nesque vitiis dediti spiritualiter corripi, et emendari,
ac veluti fraeno quodam disciplinae cohiberi : pauperes
item, et afflicti, auxilio, et consolatione pro cujusque
necessitate sublevari.   Tunc enim rite omnia et
ordine fient in Ecclesia, quum viri fideles ac pii, ad
ejus gubernationem deligentur, juxta divi Pauli prae-
scriptum, quod habetur prima ad Timotheum iii. et
Tit. i.

XXXI.   Credimus Ministros, Seniores, et Diaco-
nos debere ad functiones illas suas vocari, et promo-
veri legitima Ecclesiae electione, adhibita ad eam
seria Dei invocatione, atque eo ordine et modo qui
nobis Dei verbo praescribitur.   Debent autem im-

primis singuli cavere, ne illicitis mediis sese ad haec munia ingerant. Expectandum est enim omnibus, donec a Deo ipso vocentur, ut certum habeant vocationis suae testimonium, sciantque eam esse a Domino. Caeterum ubi sint locorum verbi Dei Ministri, eandem illi atque aequalem omnes habent tum potestatem, tum auctoritatem, ut qui sint aeque omnes Christi unici illius Episcopi universalis et capitis Ecclesiae Ministri. Porro ne sancta haec Dei ordinatio, aut violetur, aut abeat in contemptum, debent omnes de verbi Ministris et Senioribus Ecclesiae, honorifice propter opus cui incumbunt sentire, atque cum illis pacem colere; et a rixis ac contentionibus, quantum fieri potest, invicem abstinere.

XXXII. Interim credimus quidem utile esse, ut seniores qui Ecclesiis praesunt, aliquem inter se ordinem constituant, ad conservationem corporis Ecclesiae : modo studiose caveant, ne quo pacto ab iis deflectant declinentve, quae Christus ipse, unicus Magister noster, semel constituit. Nos itaque omnia humana inventa, omnesque leges rejicimus, quae ad Dei cultum sunt introductae, ut iis conscientiae ullo modo illaqueentur, aut obstringantur. Easque solas suscipimus, quae idoneae sunt, vel ad fovendam alendamque concordiam, vel ad nos in Dei obedientia retinendos. Ad id vero imprimis necessaria est excommunicatio, ex praecepto verbi Dei usurpata, et aliae illi annexae disciplinae Ecclesiasticae appendices.

APPENDIX VI

THE LAMBETH QUADRILATERAL

IN the year 1886 the Bishops of the American Church in their General Convention replied to a certain Memorial on Christian Union in the following terms :—

We, . . . do hereby solemnly declare to all whom it may concern, and especially to our fellow Christians of the different Communions in this land, who, in their several spheres, have contended for the religion of Christ:

1. Our earnest desire that the Saviour's prayer, " That we all may be one," may, in its deepest and truest sense, be speedily fulfilled;

2. That we believe that all who have been duly baptized with water, in the name of the Father, and of the Son, and of the Holy Ghost, are members of the Holy Catholic Church;

3. That in all things of human ordering or human choice relating to modes of worship and discipline, or to traditional customs, this Church is ready in the spirit of love and humility to forego all preferences of her own;

4. That this Church does not seek to absorb other Communions, but rather, co-operating with them on the basis of a common Faith and Order, to discountenance schism, to heal the wounds of the Body of Christ, and to promote the charity which is the

chief of Christian graces and the visible manifesta-
tion of Christ to the world;

But, furthermore, we do hereby affirm that the
Christian unity now so earnestly desired by the
memorialists can be restored only by the return of
all Christian communions to the principles of unity
exemplified by the undivided Catholic Church during
the first ages of its existence; which principles we
believe to be the substantial deposit of Christian
Faith and Order committed by Christ and His
Apostles to the Church unto the end of the world, and
therefore incapable of compromise or surrender by
those who have been ordained to be its stewards and
trustees for the common and equal benefit of all men.

As inherent parts of this sacred deposit, and therefore as essential to the restoration of unity among
the divided branches of Christendom, we account the
following, to wit:

1. The Holy Scriptures of the Old and New
Testament as the revealed word of God.

2. The Nicene Creed as the sufficient statement of
the Christian Faith.

3. The two Sacraments—Baptism and the Supper
of the Lord—ministered with unfailing use of
Christ's words of institution and of the elements
ordained by Him.

4. The Historic Episcopate, locally adapted in the
methods of its administration to the varying needs of
the nations and peoples called of God into the unity
of His Church.

Furthermore, Deeply grieved by the sad divisions
which affect the Christian Church in our own land,
we hereby declare our desire and readiness, so soon
as there shall be any authorized response to this
declaration, to enter into brotherly conference with
all or any Christian bodies seeking the restoration

2 F

of the organic unity of the Church, with a view to
the earnest study of the conditions under which so
priceless a blessing might happily be brought to
pass.

At the Lambeth Conference of 1888 a
Committee on Home Reunion was appointed,
which reported the above resolution of the
American bishops, and suggested that it might
become a basis of union. The Conference
afterwards adopted the following resolution :—

That, in the opinion of this Conference, the following Articles supply a basis on which approach may
be by God's blessing made towards Home Reunion :

[A] The Holy Scriptures of the Old and New
Testaments, as "containing all things necessary
to salvation," and as being the rule and ultimate
standard of faith.

[B] The Apostles' Creed, as the Baptismal
Symbol; and the Nicene Creed, as the sufficient
statement of the Christian Faith.

[C] The two Sacraments ordained by Christ
Himself—Baptism and the Supper of the Lord—
ministered with unfailing use of Christ's words of
Institution, and of the elements ordained by Him.

[D] The Historic Episcopate, locally adapted in
the methods of its administration to the varying needs
of the nations and peoples called of God into the
Unity of His Church.

It is evidently not the same thing to say
that certain things are "essential to the restoration of unity " and to make them a " basis " of
union.

APPENDIX VII

THE MANSFIELD COLLEGE CONFERENCE

IN the course of my Lectures I cited the account of the Mansfield College Conference communicated to the press in September, 1916. By the kindness of the Rev. J. H. Shakespeare I have now been supplied with the Interim Reports of four Committees on Faith, Ministry, Evangelization, and Constitution, appointed by the Conference, which were adopted by a second Conference held at Cambridge in March, 1917. From these I extract the following sections :—

A

REPORT OF THE COMMITTEE ON FAITH

Preamble.

Inasmuch as the Evangelical Free Churches of England have been led, in the good providence of God, to seek closer federation with one another for the better witness to and service of the Gospel, and inasmuch as some declaration exhibiting the substance of their common faith is desirable both as a basis of fellowship and co-operation and as a means of making known to others the truths for which these Churches stand, the following "Declaratory State-ment of Common Faith and Practice" is issued in the name of the Federation. And at the same time it is intimated as follows:—

1. The Evangelical Free Churches of England claim and cherish their place as inheritors, along with others, of the historic faith of Christendom, which found expression in the œcumenical creeds of the early and undivided Church; and this Declaratory Statement does not profess to be a comprehensive creed, but is a declaration of such truths as, in the circumstances, it seems proper to rehearse and emphasize.

2. It is an essential element in the proposals for federation that each of the federating Churches should preserve its own autonomy as regards faith and prac-tice; this statement, therefore, is not to be imposed as a disciplinary standard on any of these Churches, nor, on the other hand, does it supersede or in any way alter the place of whatever doctrinal standards any of these Churches may maintain in their con-stitution.

Declaratory Statement of Common Faith and Practice

IV

We believe that the Catholic or Universal Church is the whole company of the redeemed in heaven and on earth, and we recognize as belonging to this holy fellowship all who are united to God through faith in Christ.

The Church on earth—which is One through the Apostolic Gospel and through the living union of all its true members with its one Head, even Christ, and

which is Holy through the indwelling Holy Spirit
Who sanctifies the Body and its members—is ordained
to be the visible Body of Christ, to worship God
through Him, to promote the fellowship of His
people and the ends of His kingdom, and to go into
all the world and proclaim His Gospel for the salvation of men and the brotherhood of all mankind.   Of
this visible Church, and every branch thereof, the
only Head is the Lord Jesus Christ; and in its faith,
order, discipline, and duty, it must be free to obey
Him alone as it interprets His holy will.

B

REPORT OF THE CONSTITUTION COMMITTEE

V. *Objects.*

The following shall be the objects of the Federation :—

1. So to express the social unity in Christ of the
Evangelical Free Churches of England and to co-
ordinate their activities and resources as most effectively to promote the evangelization of the people,
and the extension of Christ's kingdom at home and
abroad.

2. To bring the Evangelical Free Churches of
England into Federal Union upon the basis of the
Evangelical faith and of the autonomy of the federa-
ting Churches.

3. To maintain liberty of conscience, and to take
action where authorized in all matters affecting the
interests, duties, rights, or privileges of the federating
Churches, when authorized to do so.

4. To enter into communion and united action
where possible with other branches of the Church
of Christ throughout the world.

PRINTED BY A. R. MOWBRAY & CO. LTD.
LONDON AND OXFORD